Reflections on Research

Reflections on Research

The Realities of Doing Research in the Social Sciences

Nina Hallowell, Julia Lawton and Susan Gregory

Open University Press

Open University Press
McGraw-Hill Education
McGraw-Hill House
Shoppenhangers Road
Maidenhead
Berkshire
England
SL6 2QL

email: enquiries@openup.co.uk
world wide web: www.openup.co.uk

and Two Penn Plaza, New York, NY 10121–2289, USA

First published 2005

A catalogue record of this book is available from the British Library

ISBN 0335 21309 X (pb) 0335 21310 3 (hb)

Library of Congress Cataloging-in-Publication Data
CIP data applied for

Typeset by RefineCatch Limited, Bungay, Suffolk
Printed in Great Britain by MPG Books Ltd, Bodmin, Cornwall

Contents

Notes on contributors

Priscilla Alderson is Professor of Childhood Studies at the Institute of Education. Her research interests include: the social construction of childhood and disability, children's rights, the new genetics, ethics and research methods. She is presently researching dilemmas in neonatal neurology and young children's role in diabetes management. Recent books include: *Institutional Rites and Rights: A Century of Childhood* (2003), *On Doing Qualitative Research Linked to Ethical Health Care* (2001) and *Young Children's Rights: Exploring Beliefs and Practice* (2000).

Kathryn Backett-Milburn is Senior Research Fellow at the Research Unit in Health, Behaviour and Change, and Co-Director of the Centre for Research on Families and Relationships, University of Edinburgh. Her research interests and publications have focused on the sociology of the family and health and illness, with a special interest in health promotion/public health. Her PhD thesis was published by Macmillan as: *Mothers and Fathers: The Development and Negotiation of Parental Behaviour*. Her current and recent research projects focus upon: children and young people; women's health; health inequalities and low-income households; food choice and eating.

Rosaline Barbour is Professor of Health and Social Care at the University of Dundee. Her current research focuses on the health-care needs of asylum seekers and the experiences of people with dysarthria and their carers. Previous work has covered professional socialization for social work and professional responses to HIV/AIDS. She co-edited *Meddling with Mythology: AIDS and the Social Construction of Knowledge* (1998) with Guro Huby, and *Developing Focus Group Research: Politics, Theory and Practice* (1999) with Jenny Kitzinger. She is currently writing a single-authored book on focus groups.

Hannah Bradby is Lecturer in Medical Sociology at Warwick University. Her research concerns health and ethnicity. A recent paper ((2003) 'Describing ethnicity in health research' *Ethnicity and Health*, 8(1): 5–13) revisits an earlier discussion of the difficulties of conceptualizing and operationalizing ethnicity in health research ((1995) Ethnicity: not a black and white issue, a research note, *Sociology of Health and Illness*, 17(3): 405–17).

Elizabeth Chapman is Research Associate at the Centre for Family Research, University of Cambridge. She is a psychologist with research interests in: cystic fibrosis (maturity and family involvement, social and ethical issues in lung transplantation, palliative care); pain management in advanced cancer and in chronic pain; and HIV and body image.

Susan Cox is Assistant Professor and Michael Smith Foundation for Health Research Scholar at The W. Maurice Young Centre for Applied Ethics, University of British Columbia. She specializes in medical sociology, bioethics and qualitative research. Her current research focuses on how new genetic knowledge and techniques reflect as well as reshape contemporary understandings of health and illness, normality and abnormality. Other interests include disability studies, interpersonal communication (in clinical and non-clinical contexts), narrative, community-based research and the role of social science methodology in ethical analysis.

Sarah Cunningham-Burley is Reader in Public Health Sciences and Co-Director of the Centre for Research on Families and Relationships at the University of Edinburgh. She has a long-standing interest in family and health research, and has been involved in many empirical studies using qualitative methods. Research relationships, whether between researchers and research participants or within research teams, have always fascinated her. As her work increasingly takes her into the realm of research management, she tries hard to make joint working a positive experience for all involved.

Gill Dunne is Senior Lecturer in the Department of Sociology at the University of Plymouth. She has written extensively on lesbian, gay and bisexual experience, with particular reference to work and family life. She is especially interested in developing the potential of non-heterosexual experience as an alternative lens for exploring the gender dynamics of inequality in the mainstream.

Susan Eley is Lecturer at the Department of Applied Social Science, University of Stirling, having worked previously as a research fellow at the University of Glasgow and at the MRC Medical Sociology Unit. She is a sociologist whose current research interests include drug use and the criminal justice system, youth justice and service provision in health and social care.

Elizabeth Ettorre is Professor of Sociology, University of Plymouth. Her research is in: the sociology of substance use; gender; bioethics; new genetics; occupational health; and mental health. She has been involved in a number of European research projects in genetics, bioethics and reproduction and has published widely in women's studies and sociology of health. Her books include: *Lesbians, Women and Society* (1980); *Women and Substance Use* (1992); *Gendered Moods* (1995) with Elianne Riska; *Women and Alcohol: A Private Pleasure or a Public Problem?* (1997); *Reproductive Genetics, Gender and the Body* (2002); *Before Birth* (2001); and *Revisioning Women and Drug Use* (forthcoming).

Catherine Exley is Lecturer in Medical Sociology in the Centre for Health Services Research, University of Newcastle upon Tyne. Her research and publications to date have focused primarily upon the organization, delivery and experience of care at the end of life. In particular, she is interested in how the roles and identities of people who are dying and their carers are negotiated and changed at this time.

Calliope (Bobbie) Farsides is Senior Lecturer in Medical Ethics at the Centre of Medical Law and Ethics, King's College, London. Her research interests are in ethical issues relating to health care, an area in which she has published widely. In recent years her main interests have been in ethical issues relating to death and dying and palliative care, and ethical issues relating to the provision and uptake of antenatal screening and testing.

Claire Foster is a chartered health psychologist. She is currently Senior Research Fellow at the Institute of Cancer Research, where she is exploring psychosocial aspects of genetic testing for breast and ovarian cancer predisposition.

Jonathan Gabe is Reader in Sociology in the Department of Social and Political Science at Royal Holloway, University of London. He has published widely in the areas of mental health, health-care professions, health policy, chronic illness, the mass media and health, and health risks. He is the editor or author of a number of books, including: *Partners in Health, Partners in Crime: Exploring the Boundaries of Criminology and Sociology of Health and Illness* (2003) (edited with Stefan Timmermans) and *Sociology of Health and Illness: A Reader* (2004) (edited with Mike Bury). He was co-editor of the journal *Sociology of Health and Illness* from 1994 to 2000.

Wendy Gnich is Research Fellow at the Research Unit in Health, Behaviour and Change, University of Edinburgh. With a disciplinary background in psychology, she has developed expertise in the evaluation of health promotion initiatives. Her recent work has included: the evaluation of initiatives focusing on tobacco use; a complex community-based initiative in a low-income area; and a national pilot programme of youth smoking cessation projects. Her research interests include: the evaluation of health promotion interventions, complex community-wide health promotion initiatives, smoking and disadvantage, youth tobacco use, mixed methods approaches to evaluation and the determinants of psychological and physical well-being throughout the life cycle.

Trudy Goodenough is Research Assistant at the Centre for Ethics in Medicine, University of Bristol. Her main research interests are in developmental psychology, health care and research with children.

Susan Gregory is Research Fellow at the Research Unit in Health, Behaviour and Change, the University of Edinburgh, where her research interests centre on the management of chronic illness in the social setting, especially within the family. She has co-edited *Gender, Power and the Household* (1999) (with Linda McKie and Sophie Bowlby). She has taught on research methods courses at the Universities of Surrey and Edinburgh, and was a member of the British Sociological Association Executive Committee (2000–03). She is currently co-book review editor for *Sociology of Health and Illness* and sits on the Lothian Research Ethics Committee.

Rachel Grellier is currently working for Options Consultancy Services (or 'a consultancy company') as Assistant Health and Social Development Specialist. Her work largely focuses on HIV/AIDS impact and mitigation, livelihoods, and gender issues; working with national governments, non-governmental organizations and civil society in developing countries and with international donor organizations.

Nina Hallowell teaches Social Science and Ethics in Public Health Sciences, the Medical School, University of Edinburgh. She has published widely on the social and ethical implications of new genetic technologies. She has been a member of three ethics committees, and is regularly involved in running training workshops for ethics committee members.

Khim Horton is Lecturer (clinical) at the European Institute of Health and Medical Sciences, University of Surrey. She is a qualified nurse with specialist expertise in the care of older people. She is Pathway Leader on the MSc in Advanced Practice and focuses her teaching in gerontological studies and research methodologies. She works closely with local Primary Care Trusts, developing work in the management of falls among older people. Her previous work includes research on accidents among ethnic minority older people, as well as among people with Parkinsons disease.

Julie Kent is Senior Lecturer in Sociology at the University of the West of England. Her recent research has looked at the regulation and governance of medical devices and human tissue engineered products; ethical protection in genetic epidemiology; and women in science. Her publications include *Social Perspectives on Pregnancy and Childbirth for Midwives, Nurses and the Caring Professions* (2000).

Julia Lawton is based at the Research Unit in Health, Behaviour and Change, the University of Edinburgh, where her research remit is 'health-related risks and lifestyles'. Prior to this, she held a Junior Research Fellowship at Newnham College, University of Cambridge. She is a social anthropologist, who gained both her undergraduate degree and PhD from Cambridge University. She is the author of *The Dying Process: Patients' Experiences of Palliative Care* (2000), and she was awarded the New Writer's Prize by *Sociology of Health and Illness* for an article published in 1998. She has published extensively in the following areas: lay experiences of type 2 diabetes; patients' experiences of palliative care; and the ethical issues arising from qualitative research.

Abby Lippman is Professor in the Department of Epidemiology and Bio-statistics at McGill University. Combining activism with research, she is on the Advisory Board of the US-based Council for Responsible Genetics and co-chairs the Canadian Women's Health Network. She is on the Steering Committee of the Health Canada-funded Working Group on Women and Health Protection. Her research has centred on feminist studies of applied genetic technologies, focusing on general issues in, and the politics of, women's health, and paying specific attention to the relation of gender to health in the areas of biotechnology and health (care) reform policies.

Liz Lobb has a PhD in Psychological Medicine and a Masters in Applied Science (Behavioural Science) from the University of Sydney, Australia. Her research interests and publications are in the areas of communicating prognosis in early stage and metastatic breast cancer, and genetic counselling in familial breast/ovarian cancer. In 2003, she was awarded a four-year NH&MRC Post Doctoral Australian Clinical Research Fellowship. She spent the first year as Research Fellow in the Hereditary Cancer Clinic at Prince of Wales Hospital and is now based at Edith Cowan University in Perth collaborating in familial cancer and palliative care research.

Lesley Lockyer is Senior Lecturer in the Faculty of Health and Social Care, University of the West of England. She qualified as a nurse in 1980 and worked in a number of cardiac units through the 1980s. From 1990, she began working as a research nurse in a cardiac unit. Her research interest in women and coronary heart disease developed during this time, and in 1995 she began a doctorate exploring women's experiences of coronary heart disease in the Department of Social and Political Science, Royal Holloway College. Her research continues in this area, focusing on decision-making and cardiac rehabilitation.

Alice Lovell retired from a senior lecturer post at South Bank University in 2000. She teaches psychology at Birkbeck College, Faculty of Continuing Education. She has carried out research on the impact of miscarriage, still-birth and early neonatal death on bereaved parents and on medical and religious professionals. Her other research includes evaluating the effects of giving expectant mothers their own maternity case notes and studying access to general practitioners.

Marion McAllister is a Macmillan Genetic Counsellor and Honorary Lecturer at the North West Genetics Knowledge Park (Nowgen) and Regional Genetics Service/Academic Unit of Medical Genetics, St Mary's Hospital, Manchester. She has clinical and research expertise in the area of inherited cancers. Trained as a social scientist, she completed her PhD at the Centre for Family Research, University of Cambridge. Her 'theory of engagement' provides an explanation for variation in behaviour around pre-dictive genetic testing for a hereditary cancer syndrome. She has recently been appointed to a new post within the Nowgen Valuation and Evaluation of Genetic Counselling research theme.

Richard Mitchell is Research Fellow in the Research Unit in Health, Behaviour and Change (RUHBC), University of Edinburgh. He joined RUHBC as a member of the core research staff in January 2001, having previously worked at the Centre for Longitudinal Studies in London, and the geography departments of Bristol and Leeds Universities. His research interests are spatial inequalities in health (with particular reference to heart disease); the design, implementation and evaluation of policies and strategies to tackle health inequalities; and quantitative/geographical research method-ologies. He is co-author of the textbook *Health, Place and Society* (2001).

Virginia Morrow is Research Lecturer at the Child-Focused Research Centre, Department of Health and Social Care, Brunel University, London. Her research interests include qualitative research methods and the ethics of social research; the history and sociology of childhood; social capital; child labour; children's perspectives on their environments; and children's rights. Recent research has explored the relationship between social capital and health for children and young people – see *Networks and Neighbourhoods: Children's and Young People's Perspectives* (2001), Health Development Agency, London.

Melissa Nash undertook her doctoral research at the Department of Anthropology, University College, London. Her PhD, which was awarded in 2002, is entitled: 'The 'arts' as cultural intervention for people with learning disabilities: A voluntary sector 'community' initiative in south-east London'. Her research interests are in medical anthropology, disability theory, performance theory and gender studies.

Odette Parry is Professor of Social Welfare and Community Justice and Head of the Social Inclusion Research Unit (SIRU) at NEWI, the University of Wales. Her main research interests are the sociology of education and health. Peer-reviewed journals in which her recent research findings are published include *Sociology, Addiction, British Medical Journal, Health Education Research and Health Promotion International*.

Stephen Platt is the Director of the Research Unit in Health, Behaviour and Change, University of Edinburgh. He has been active as a social and health researcher for nearly 30 years. Although trained as a medical sociologist, he has conducted research using theoretical, conceptual and methodological tools from other disciplines, including social policy, psychology, anthropology, economics and epidemiology. His current research interests include: investigating the health impact of organizational change and restructuring; social and cultural aspects of suicidal behaviour; evaluation of complex interventions for health improvement; smoking and socio-economic disadvantage; and supporting practice and policy development relating to public mental health and well-being (particularly at the community level).

Laura Potts is Senior Lecturer in the School of Management, Community and Communication at York St John College, York. The main focus of her research is the environmental risk, and prevention, of breast cancer, and the legitimacy of citizen expertise in relation to this. She has published in academic and popular health journals, and maintains an engagement as an activist involved in UK and US campaign networks. She edited *Ideologies of Breast Cancer: Feminist Perspectives* (2000). Other research interests include (auto)biography and the politics of food.

Shirley Prendergast was Reader in Research at Anglia Polytechnic University, Cambridge. During an extensive research career her interests and writing have focused on young people in relation to parenthood, sexuality, schooling, health and the body. Her most recent work includes a study of teenage pregnancy funded by Joseph Rowntree and an Economic and Social Research Council funded project with Gill Dunne on transitions for lesbian and gay young people.

Martin Richards is the Director of the Centre for Family Research, University of Cambridge. His research interests include psychosocial aspects of the new human genetics and marriage, divorce and family life. He is a member of the Human Genetics Commission and is currently working on a book on the history and future of human genetic manipulation and reproductive technologies. Recent books include: *Body Lore and Laws* (edited with Andrew Bainham and Shelley Day-Sclater) and *Children and their Families* (edited with Andrew Bainham, Bridget Lindley and Liz Trinder).

Deborah Ritchie is Senior Lecturer in Health Promotion at Queen Margaret University College. She has significant experience of working as a practitioner and as an academic in public health/health promotion. Much of her research has focused on smoking cessation. She was involved in the Breathing Space Project which aimed to produce a significant shift in community norms towards non-smoking in a low-income area in Edinburgh. Her current research aims to evaluate the effectiveness of a culturally attuned method of supporting smoking cessation in a low-income community, through a narrative analysis, and process and impact evaluation.

Ann Robertson is Associate Professor in the Department of Public Health Sciences at the University of Toronto. Her most recent research is a study comparing discourses on genetic risk for breast cancer in Canadian print media, popular science journals and policy documents related to genetic testing for late-onset disease. From October 2002 to June 2003, she was Visiting Scholar at the Centre for Family Research at Cambridge, having received a Career Transition Award from the Canadian Institutes of Health Research (CIHR) Institute of Genetics to study issues at the intersection of genetics, bioethics and public health.

Susan Robinson is Research Associate in the Department of General Practice at King's College, London. She is a sociologist whose research interests include chronic illness, evaluation of health service initiatives, the experience of overseas GPs in the NHS and outcome measures for counselling in general practice.

Tom Shakespeare is Director of Outreach at PEALS, a University of Newcastle-based research centre promoting research and debate on the social and ethical aspects of genetics. Most of his research has been in the field of disability studies, and his books include *The Sexual Politics of Disability* (1996).

Hilary Thomas is Senior Lecturer in the Department of Sociology, University of Surrey. Her research interests include the sociology of health and illness, the sociology of the body and time, and the sociology of reproduction and women's health. She was convenor of the British Sociological Association Medical Sociology Group (1991–94) and President of the European Society for Health and Medical Sociology (1999–2003).

Stefan Timmermans is Associate Professor at Brandeis University, Massachusetts. His research interests include medical technologies, and death and dying. He has published *Sudden Death and the Myth of CPR* (1999) and *The Gold Standard: The Challenge of Evidence-Based Medicine and Standardization in Health Care* (2003). He is currently completing a book on forensic medicine.

Kay Tisdall is Senior Lecturer in Social Policy at the University of Edinburgh. Her current research topics are diverse, linked by: methodological interests in research with children; theoretical interests in participation, collaboration and rights; and policy interests in 'joined up' policy, particularly in relation to disability and children. Current and recent research projects include local government expenditure on child poverty, the views of children in family law proceedings, and cross-country comparisons of policies affecting disabled children. She is Programme Director for the interdisciplinary MSc in Childhood Studies.

Jonathan Tritter is Research Director of the Institute of Governance and Public Management, University of Warwick. His main research interests relate to the relationship between patients, carers and the health professionals who treat them, particularly in relation to the experience of cancer. He is Convenor of the Sociology of Cancer Study Group and has published *Improving Cancer Services through Patient Involvement* (2003), with Norma Daykin, Simon Evans and Michail Sanidas.

Julia Twigg is Professor of Social Policy and Sociology at the University of Kent. Her current main interests are the body, ageing and social care. She has written extensively on family carers and their support, in *Carers Perceived: Policy and Practice in Informal Care*; the constitution of personal care, in *Bathing – the Body and Community Care*; and the role of the body in public policy, in *The Social Politics of the Body: Food, Health and Social Care*.

Clare Williams is Research Fellow in the Department of Midwifery and Women's Health, King's College, London. She holds a postdoctoral Wellcome Trust Biomedical Ethics Fellowship exploring whether perceptions of the foetus are changing, and what the possible clinical, ethical, social and policy implications of this might be. Her current research interests include genetics, biomedical ethics, gender and chronic illness. She has published a number of papers in these areas and has also published a book on teenagers' management of chronic illness, entitled *Mothers, Young People and Chronic Illness* (2002).

Emma Williamson is Wellcome Trust Research Fellow for the EPEG Project, Centre for Ethics in Medicine, University of Bristol. The EPEG project is concerned with participants' perspectives on ethical protection within genetic epidemiological research. Her current research interests include: domestic violence and health; ethics of research and participation; research methodologies; ethics and genetic research; gender and technologies; children and research; and feminist action-orientated research.

Acknowledgements

Without the help and support of many individuals, this book would never have seen the light of day. We would like to start by thanking our original editor, Jacinta Evans, who had confidence in our idea for the book and helped us to secure a contract. Thanks are also due to our current editor, Rachel Gear, who continued to encourage and support us following Jacinta's departure. We are indebted to all of our contributors, but in particular Ginny Morrow, who provided much-needed feedback on the final chapter, and Odette Parry, who was, as always, tremendously supportive and a great listener. We are also very grateful to Margaret MacPhee who provided excellent secretarial support in the final stages of the book's production.

Finally, Nina would like to thank all the staff of Favorit in Teviot Place, who kept her supplied with pieces of cake and cups of good coffee throughout the months she sat there editing, summarizing and writing the bits around the edges.

Julia Lawton and Susan Gregory are based in the Research Unit in Health, Behaviour and Change at Edinburgh University, which is jointly funded by the Chief Scientist Office and NHS Health Scotland. The views expressed in this book are not necessarily those of these funding bodies.

1
Research in practice, or doing the business

This book is concerned with the day-to-day realities of doing social science research. It is based upon the reflections and experiences of a wide range of established social researchers, the majority of whom undertake research in the field of health care. By drawing upon their accounts of setting up research projects, negotiating access, collecting data, and disseminating findings, the book highlights a multitude of practical and ethical complexities involved in the conduct of empirically based research. It delineates the emotional, social and cultural factors involved at various stages of the research process, and sets this in the context of wider debates about the relationship between research methods and research ethics.

Reader: Oh no! Not another boring research methods book!

Editors: Stop. Calm down and DO NOT PANIC. Yes, this is a research methods book, but it is no ordinary research methods book. This is a 'how it went' book, rather than a 'how to do it' book. It is a book of real-life research stories. As such, this book will not tell you how to actually do research, although it might give you some idea of what not to do or how to get out of a sticky situation. It is our belief that research is a bit like bike-riding – nothing quite improves one's skills as much as actually doing it. But of course before you start riding that bike it is often quite useful to get some tips about your journey, such as which are the best routes to take or which pubs/cake shops you should incorporate into the itinerary. Well, in some senses this book is to novice (and even long in the tooth) researchers what the Lonely Planet is to bike riders – it is a book of research journeys; and we hope you will enjoy reading about these excursions or forays in the world of social science research.

Everything you ever wanted to know about research, but were never told

In recent years, the way we talk about social science research has changed. As Seale notes, when it comes to writing up our research reports 'method-ological self consciousness' has become the norm (1999: 159). Authors are more willing than ever before to acknowledge that empirical research, particularly qualitative research, is a ' . . . complex, often chaotic, sometimes messy, even conflictual . . . ' (Byrne-Armstrong *et al.* 2001: vii) endeavour. However, despite what could be called the 'reflexive turn' in research report-ing, the realities of doing empirical research are generally glossed over in methods textbooks, research reports and journal articles, which still provide fairly sanitized accounts of the research process. Whilst problems are alluded to and emotions are sometimes 'written in', the nature of the chaos, and the degree of angst experienced along the way, are frequently lost in the report-ing. A cursory glance suggests that, in most cases, research projects generally run like clockwork, that researchers enter 'the field', collect masses of interest-ing data, encounter no problems (of any kind) *en route*, return to their offices and churn out a range of fascinating papers, get promoted and live happily ever after. Would that this really was the case. Just scratch away at the surface and catch these researchers in an unguarded moment – at postgraduate training and support events or in the bar following presentations at confer-ences – and the truth will eventually out. It is in these private spaces that the difficulties and compromises, as well as the joys, that are inherent in most research projects are shared and discussed.

By focusing upon the real-life research stories of real-life researchers, this book aims to redress the balance. Our hope is that it will give you some insight into the perils, pitfalls and pleasures that researchers really experience when undertaking empirical research in the social sciences.

Genesis: in the beginning there was the conversation

As with many good ideas, the way that this book came into being was during a chance conversation over a cup of tea (and quite a few biscuits), which took place not long after Julia and Sue had started new research jobs in Edinburgh. We were just chatting about some of the stranger experiences we had had during the course of our research careers. We realized, as a result of talking to our colleagues over the years, that we were not the only researchers who had stories to tell of frankly bizarre and strange happenings, and we bemoaned the fact that such accounts rarely gained the light of day in publications. At this point Julia raised the idea of a book she had been discussing with Nina. Nina had long threatened that she would write an article about smoking as a methodological tool, and both she and Julia had fantasized about writing a real-life research book. This would be a book full of stories that reflected the 'nitty gritty' of doing social research: stories that everyone had, but were never quite prepared to tell in their more 'official' publications. At that moment, both Sue and Julia thought, 'why don't we just bite the bullet and do it?', and before long the germ of an idea that resulted in this book became a reality, and Nina was granted her wish to publish a piece, albeit a small one, on smoking.

In the spirit of the book, the following section is an account of the perils, pitfalls and pleasures of putting together and editing a collection of this sort. It outlines how we did it and what we learned from doing it. Sadly, we do not have the space to tell you what we wish we had done differently!

Exodus: the journey towards a contract and a manuscript

During our first meeting, the three of us drew up a long list of people we knew who had stories to tell, and some whom we thought might be prepared to bare all. As we talked, we became more and more excited about the idea: we were convinced the book was publishable and realized that we needed a plan of action.

Our first move was to sound out both publishers and potential contributors. This was also the first obstacle we encountered. Publishers normally require a clear and reasonably comprehensive proposal before they will seriously consider an idea. It gets worse: before they will consider issuing a contract, they require a detailed outline which assesses both the potential market and the competition and which, most importantly, meticulously details the content of each and every chapter. When you are the sole author of a book, the latter task is fairly straightforward (at least in theory); however, when you have a large number of contributors, as we proposed to have, it is more of an uphill struggle. We were in a Catch 22 situation: we had to get our contributors on board with a vague promise of a book contract, whilst at the same time get a publisher interested, with what can only be described as a vague idea of what the finished product would look like. Undaunted, we capitalized on our attendance at a medical sociology conference in 2001 to implement a two-pronged recruitment strategy. First, we approached fellow researchers to sound out their willingness to get involved. Much charm and (implicit and explicit) coercion was involved in this stage of the recruitment drive. We described the book as a 'warts and all' collection – a 'kiss and tell' book – and were pleasantly surprised by their level of interest. Perhaps the promise of a publication, which required little in the way of effort (we only wanted pieces of between 500 and 2000 words), fuelled their enthusiasm? Plus, of course, their recognition that our proposed book was needed, especially on the research methods courses they were teaching.

Armed with the promise of about 20 research stories, we then approached two editors who were attending the conference. We reckoned, and previous experience had taught us, that nothing boosts a publisher's interest in a book proposal better than the thought of competition, so these conversations or 'pitches' were peppered with heavy hints that 'X from Y publishers is very enthusiastic about this idea'. (Incidentally, previous experience has also taught us that nothing gets a door slammed in your face more quickly than letting it slip that your proposed book is based upon a PhD dissertation – so be warned.) On this occasion our strategy seemed to work. By the end of the conference, we had expressions of interest from two publishers.

We went home and emailed all our potential contributors asking them to send us an abstract of between 100 and 200 words which captured the essence of the real-life research story they had intimated they might divulge. We were initially concerned that they would all opt to share their doom and gloom stories, and that, if this were the case, novice researchers who read our book might conclude that research is such a difficult and depressing affair that they would radically rethink their career choices. So, in order to produce a book which would give a balanced perspective, we suggested that contributors might like to consider writing about the 'pleasures' of doing research rather than just the 'perils'. Furthermore, we recommended that if they did choose to write about a problem, they should also consider detailing the ways in which they attempted to resolve it. We sat back and waited.

Clearly the idea of the book had captured our colleagues' imagination: the abstracts began to roll in thick and fast, our inboxes started filling up and, before too long, we had amassed over 40 ideas for stories. We now faced the second hurdle: how to actually organize this apparently disparate material and come up with a recognizable and, more importantly, tight and marketable book proposal. Independently, we read all the abstracts and searched for themes that would allow us to structure the book in a logical and appealing way. We brought the fruits of our thematic analyses to an editorial meeting and hammered out our ideas. After some (at times heated) discussions, the key themes were agreed upon, and the real work began. We researched our competitors, assessed the potential markets, and wrote the outline, a quite daunting task given that initially we had only requested 100 to 200 word summaries from our contributors. Once satisfied with the content, we worked on the form of the proposal, and, when all the t's were crossed and i's dotted, we sent it off, sat back and crossed our fingers. Some months later, revisions were submitted and contracts were signed, and we got back to our contributors with instructions to start writing. Then it hit us – we had to produce a book within 12 months; a book which had over 40 contributors; a book which would probably stretch our organizational skills and powers of persuasion to their limits.

What you cannot appreciate is how much work, heartache and emotional blackmail has gone into producing these pages. It is not only the three of us who have put in the effort, though; all of our contributors also had to work towards our tight deadlines. In some cases, they have put up with our (at times) very heavy editorial hands. Others were subjected to threats such as 'no coffee breaks with me' or, worse still, 'no gossip about the department' until they delivered. Baring their souls was difficult for some, and we hope that they have found this experience, if not enjoyable, at least cathartic. Throughout the process, all our contributors behaved with professionalism, many have bitten their tongues at some of our more outlandish editorial suggestions and (nearly) all delivered the goods on time. We cannot thank them enough for their forbearance, good cheer and, ultimately, for making this book happen.

We hope that you find reading this book enjoyable and useful. For those of you who have not yet entered 'the field', we hope that reading it gives you some insight into what it is really like out there. For those of you who are already out there, it may give you some comfort to know that you are not alone: we have all been there, done that, and many of us have the scars to prove it.

Revelation: what is to come

The way in which this book is structured emerged from the contributions we received, not *vice versa*. You are probably thinking that giving our contributors a free reign to write about anything they wanted was a little foolhardy. Indeed, there were times whilst we waited for their stories to make their way through the ether when we thought, 'Oh no, maybe we should have been more directive'. However, the idea underlying this project was 'to tell it like it really is', so in that spirit we left our contributors to it and just waited to see what casting our net so widely would bring in. Luckily for us, this strategy seems to have worked, for it generated a range of stories that, in our experience, are broadly representative of the issues likely to be of importance to social researchers in general, and to new researchers in particular.

In some senses, the structure of this book is arbitrary – whilst we have organized the contributions into four different chapters, these chapters should not be read as mutually exclusive. In reality, Emotions, Self, Others and Control constitute a series of cross-cutting themes which are emphasized to a greater or lesser degree in each and every story. Thus, all of the vignettes in this collection could be read through an emotional lens or as an illustration of control *et cetera*. However, clearly the book would have been a more difficult read if we had not imposed some structure upon the stories contained herein. Therefore, whilst most of the contributions contain elements of all four themes, some address individual themes more explicitly than others and the vignettes have been organized into chapters on this basis.

Chapter 2, Emotions, brings together a group of vignettes in which researchers reflect upon the emotional aspects of their work. Whilst we have long accepted that researchers and research participants are first and foremost 'active subjects', who not only affect but also are affected by research, the extent to which the latter is really the case is rarely discussed in any depth. The research stories contained in this chapter forcefully debunk the myth that research in the social sciences is an objective and emotionally detached process. In reflecting upon their feelings, the contributors demonstrate that research involves a great deal of emotional work, and, at one and the same time, can be experienced as lonely, gruelling, rewarding and mesmerizing.

The third chapter, Self, deals with the issue of self-presentation and its impact upon the research process. When gathering data face to face, researchers frequently rely upon building rapport between themselves and their research participants (for a critique of this position, see Dunscombe and Jessop 2002). How do we go about this? What things do we, or should we, take into consideration? Is it really necessary to like, or be liked by, our research participants? The research situation itself is an anomalous situation, a situation that is characterized by differences in power and expertise. How do we get around this; indeed, should we even try? The stories in this chapter suggest that paying attention to our physical appearance and behaviour can play a pivotal role in generating a sense of trust between ourselves and our research participants. But how far should we be prepared to go?

The vignettes in Chapter 4, Others, highlight the ways in which social science research, for better or for worse, is ultimately an endeavour that involves other people. Each of the contributors reflect on the role and influence of others at different points in the research process, from before one enters the field to long after the data are secured and dissemination is underway. By documenting the ways in which the interests of various parties (fellow researchers, gatekeepers, research participants, the press, and so on) feed into the research agenda and influence outputs in both negative and positive ways, the vignettes in this chapter put paid to the myth that research is a lone endeavour.

The fifth chapter tackles the issue of Control. The vignettes in this chapter suggest that the balance of power within the research situation is not necessarily as clear-cut as we may think. The theme underlying all the contributions in this chapter is control: who has it and how it is negotiated. The contributors detail ways in which participants and researchers alike, gain, maintain or even lose control during the period of data gathering. They also demonstrate that, above all else, researching people's lives requires a degree of trust and reciprocity, although we can question the extent to which this is desirable, or at times even ethical (Dunscombe and Jessop 2002).

Whilst we hope that these research vignettes make for an enjoyable read and give you some invaluable tips for carrying out your own research, at the heart of this book there lies a serious message. Although most of the contributions are ostensibly very different in both their form and content, they can also be read as illustrating a common underlying theme: namely, that research is necessarily a moral activity. These vignettes illustrate that, as researchers, we are involved in making ethical decisions at each and every stage of the research process, whether it be writing proposals, negotiating access, gathering and analysing data, or disseminating findings.

The idea that social research is necessarily a moral or ethical activity (Homan 1991; Plummer 2001) is explored in the final chapter of this book, which focuses upon the relationship between research methods and research ethics. We argue that not only have discussions of research methods become objectified and abstracted from research practice, but that a similar trend can be observed in discussions of research ethics (Plummer 2001; Edwards and Mauthner 2002). We outline recent debates concerning the need for research governance in the social sciences, and examine arguments for, and against, the adoption of a quasi-medical model of research ethics – one which specifically focuses on a limited number of tried and trusted ethical issues, such as consent and confidentiality.

Reflecting upon the earlier chapters, we argue that research raises ethical dilemmas at every turn; dilemmas that may not, or cannot, be predicted in advance, and are not necessarily amenable to *a priori* categorization as issues concerning consent and confidentiality. In other words, the complex moral dilemmas that arise in practice, and that often require instant resolution, bear little resemblance to the abstract (re)formulation of ethical issues so beloved by research ethics committees and bioethicists alike.

Finally, we call for a reconceptualization of the relationship between research ethics and research methods. Social science research, like any human activity, is a moral activity, and should be acknowledged as such. We suggest that what makes research 'ethical' is not independent scrutiny by an ethics committee, following a set of abstract principles, or the researcher having 'good' intentions, it is what we actually do in the field that counts. As the vignettes collected in this book so vividly illustrate, in social science, as in life, actions frequently speak louder than words.

Acts or, rather, omissions

Before we turn to the vignettes themselves, it is necessary to point out that certain aspects of research in the social sciences are less well represented in the following chapters than others. Whilst we tried to avoid any omissions, in the end the book's content was dependent upon who finally contributed and what they wanted to, or were willing to, write about.

From the outset, we recognized that different issues might arise in quantitative and qualitative research, thus we made a concerted effort to invite contributors from different methodological backgrounds and in different fields. However, as you will see, many, but by no means all, of our contributions have come from qualitative researchers working in the field of health care. This is a reflection of our (the editors') research preoccupations, and hence our networks, and so should not be taken as an indication that qualitative research potentially generates more interesting stories than quantitative research, because quite clearly it does not (see Platt, Chapter 4; and Mitchell, Chapter 4). Nor do we want to suggest that research in the field of health care creates more dilemmas, or is more pleasurable, than research in other fields, because quite patently this is not the case (see Dunne, Chapter 4; Morrow, Chapter 5; and Tritter, Chapter 4).

Whilst a minority of our contributors have focused upon some of the unforeseen pleasures of undertaking research, as we predicted, the majority, despite our exhortations to 'think up-beat and discuss the pleasures', chose to reflect upon the problems they had encountered during their research careers (perhaps disorder and escalating chaos make for better stories?) But, as we had asked, they have also attempted to describe how these problems were resolved, and so the book contains quite a few handy tips, should you find yourself in a similar situation.

Perhaps inevitably, most of our contributors have chosen to focus upon the more practical aspects of research, in particular the data-gathering and dissemination phases of the research process. Upon reflection, this was also to be expected, as arguably, in our experience at least, it is going out into the field and engaging with research participants or dealing with journalists that usually generates the most interesting stories, and on occasion the most intense moral dilemmas. Perhaps disappointingly none of our contributors chose to write about trying to secure funding[1] or data analysis. Whilst we are not surprised that no one wrote about generating research income – for, after all, who wants their innermost feelings about various grant-awarding bodies/sponsors to go down in print? – we were disappointed that no one wrote about their experiences of wrestling with SPPS-x or doing Grounded Theory. Data analysis, as we all know, is an altogether more lonely process (see Exley, Chapter 2). Furthermore, like all intellectual endeavours, it is a fairly idiosyncratic skill, which, to a certain extent, defies description. How often have you read papers that detail at great length the analytic procedures used and still want to ask 'how did they really do that, or why did they make that decision about the analysis and not another one?' Whilst the use of computer packages such as NUD*IST, Atlas-ti and SPSS-x suggest that we are all in the process of standardizing our analytic procedures, in reality both qualitative and quantitative data analysis is primarily dependent upon the choices, decisions and interpretations of individuals. Whether it involves teamwork or a lone researcher, data analysis is largely an invisible process, which is all in the mind, or minds, of researchers (Doucet and Mauthner 2002: 129). Maybe it is just too difficult to write research stories about these often fleeting mental processes?

In order to fill these gaps, we considered whether we as editors should produce some vignettes that described our dealings with funders/sponsors, writing a proposal or analysing data, for we all had stories to tell of opening rejection letters, reading decidedly unfair (in our opinion) reviews of our proposals, being drowned in data, of sleepless nights as we tossed and turned thinking about how we might pay the mortgage when our contract ended, or how to interpret our data. However, we felt we should really keep our contributions to a minimum. So, whilst we would have loved to have spilt the beans ourselves, or for some of our contributors to have written about the triumphs and tribulations of grant generation and data analysis, in the final event no one did. Maybe these issues should be the focus of the next two books?

P.S.

Writing this book together meant that we had to come to an agreement about many stylistic issues. The one that generated one of the most fraught debates was how we should refer to the people who are the focus of research in our commentary. Should we opt for 'participants', 'informants', 'respondents', 'research subjects' or 'the researched'? All of these terms carry differing connotations; some are commonly interpreted as objectifying those who take part in research (such as 'research subject', 'the researched'), whilst others imply some degree of active involvement in the research process (for example, 'respondent', 'participant') (see Oliver 2003, Chapter 1, for a cogent summary of the naming debate). Nina favoured using the term 'subject' on the grounds that, whilst researchers may like to think that the people who take part in their research are active participants, in most cases they are not (Birch and Miller 2002). She also argued that the term 'subject' is used in other contexts to connote active subjectivity and agency, and therefore need not necessarily be read in a negative way. Furthermore, she pointed out that, on occasion, individuals actively resist researchers and try to subvert the research process (see Chapter 5), and therefore can be seen as 'active subjects' not the 'passive objects' of research. However, both Sue and Julia felt that the tradition of using 'subject' within empiricist research has meant that this term, at least in the context of writings about research methods, normally objectifies those who are the focus of research and implies 'passivity', an implication with which they were very unhappy. They wanted to use a term which would emphasize our conviction that those who take part in research are active agents (even if the research in which they are involved provides them with little scope for exercising their agency) and have the right to be treated as such by researchers. Thus, as democracy rules, it was agreed to use 'research participant', a term Sue and Julia thought more evocative of these sentiments, throughout our commentary. However, we would like you to note that in many ways this is a compromise, for we are aware that the nomenclature in this area is imperfect. We would also like you to bear in mind that any term that researchers use to refer to their participants/subjects/respondents *et cetera* has political and ethical overtones, and therefore can be read in a myriad of ways. So with this potential confusion cleared up, let's get on with the business in hand.

Note

1   For those of you who are interested in learning more about how to put together a (qualitative) grant proposal, we suggest you take a look at the special issue of *Qualitative Health Research* published in July 2003 (Vol. 3, No. 6), which tackles this subject.

2
Emotions

As various commentators have recently observed, when researchers write about their research experiences, they tend to confine themselves to questions of access or technical rigour, or they focus on the effects of the research on their research participants (for example Hubbard *et al.* 2001; Johnson and Clarke 2003). With few notable exceptions (such as Cannon 1989; Kleinman and Copp 1993), researchers have remained very silent when it comes to talking about how they felt when they undertook their research.[1] Yet, as the vignettes in this chapter demonstrate, it is time we put paid to the popular conception that research can be, and is, an objective and emotionally detached process. Emotional issues – for ourselves as well as our research participants – can arise at many different points in the research process (and indeed, beyond it) and in many different guises. And, just as research can be a pleasurable and exciting experience, it can also be distressing and emotionally isolating. It may also require considerable 'emotion work' (Hochschild 1983) on our part in order to gain the confidence and trust necessary to put our study participants at their ease (Cannon 1989), and to recognize and deal with any problems that may arise.

The sorrows and joys of doing research: engaging and disengaging

The chapter opens with a piece by Hilary Thomas, which raises a number of issues relevant to the chapter as whole. Thomas shares some of the lessons she learned in her first ever interview study which explored women's sexual, reproductive and contraceptive experiences. At an early stage in the project, Thomas decided to schedule three interviews on the same morning, a decision that, as she vividly recounts, proved a big mistake. The first two women she interviewed raised highly emotive issues that Thomas had not anticipated, and which shocked and distressed her to such an extent that, by the time she arrived at the last interview, she was too emotionally drained to do a competent job. In sharing this story, Thomas not only warns of the dangers of trying to do too many interviews in too short a space of time, she also draws our attention to the notion that there may be no such thing as a 'safe' question.

Hard labour

Hilary Thomas

One bright morning in 1979, I set out to conduct interviews for my PhD research, a qualitative interview study of women's experiences of contraception. I had booked three interviews to complete that morning and was feeling hopeful of a good morning's work. By lunchtime, I was back in my college room, a few hours older and several researcher-years wiser.

I was a young, novitiate research student and this was my first interview study. The production of experiential data about women's sexual, contraceptive and reproductive histories was fairly unusual at that time, with most sociology of reproduction concentrating on the experience of childbirth, and the sociology of fertility on the (mis)matching of intentions and eventual family size. I was therefore aware that the interviews might be difficult for my respondents, however sensitively I approached the subject matter. I anticipated that the women might feel more comfortable talking about pregnancy and birth than their experiences of sex and contraception.

By the morning in question, I had completed 16 interviews, nearly a third of my target. It felt like it was time to step up the pace – to get on with it and arrange interviews closer together in order to use my time more efficiently. In short, my thoughts that morning were probably more focused on work rates than on the content of the interviews.

The interview checklist was designed to guide both the respondent and myself into the intimate areas of sexual and contraceptive experience via initial questions about sex education and menstruation. The term 'having sex' was introduced into each interview in the question, 'Can you remember when you first wanted to have sex with someone which may not have been when you first did?' It followed the questions about sex education and menstruation and marked the start of the main part of the interview. It was worded in this way partly to avoid the rather bald 'How old were you when you first had sex?', but also to encourage women to recall times when they might have wished to have had sex but for some reason did not. In my head, then, this design allowed for some fairly unproblematic questions about learning about sex, before I raised what I assumed would be the more sensitive issue of sexual experience. This had worked well in earlier interviews, as indicated by interviewees' laughter when school sex education lessons were recalled.

My first interview that morning was with a woman I named Frances. She explained that a change of secondary school had meant that she had missed most of the (limited) sex education available. Her mother had explained about periods. I asked about learning about sexual intercourse:

Frances: Yes, well, I'll explain to you, now. It's not a very nice way of finding out. I had a stepfather and he was a bit – I don't know – and he used to go into great detail about things like that – he was a bit strange. So I learned then. He was a bit funny – thank goodness he's not around any longer! It's a terrible way to find out . . .

HT: Was that something he talked to just you about?

Frances: Yes, he'd wait till my Mum was out . . . He put it in such *vulgar* terms – it's enough to put anyone off . . . it wasn't a very pleasant way to find out . . . luckily I met my husband when I was 15 and of course once we got to know each other pretty well, I used to ask him! (laughs)

I pressed on, a bit shocked by these responses to my 'safe' questions. I was vaguely aware that I did not want the interview to 'stir up' experiences and emotions that she might in retrospect have wished to have kept unvoiced. Coming to the questions about having sex, Frances explained that she had been very close to her boyfriend, whom she met when she was 15 and later married. She felt that she had been able to talk to him, but delayed having sex because she was still frightened of her stepfather. There was, as readers sitting in the 21st century will probably have guessed, a more complicated reason behind her fear:

Frances: Well, the thing is I was . . . um . . . about 13½, as I said, when I was 14 he explained about sex, but before then he did try and attempt to have sexual intercourse with me. I was 13½, very young . . .

HT: Did you manage to fend him off?

Frances: Oh, yeah, because my mother always came back. But I was so frightened of him 'cause he used to knock both of us about. I didn't dare tell anyone . . . And later on I did get brave enough to tell my mother about it and she said, "Why on earth didn't you tell me?" And I said, "Well things were bad enough at the time",' I mean, *she* was having problems. But a childhood experience like that at that age – it really does frighten you!

In her account, she constantly juxtaposed and compared the behaviour of her stepfather, the need to protect her mother and her lack of support from all around, including her school, where bruises were noticed and noted but no effective action was taken, with the strength she found in her relationship with her boyfriend. Re-reading the transcript in 2002, I note in the above exchange that my question 'Did you manage to fend him off?' may have directed her towards an account that sex with her stepfather did not happen. Rather than an open question 'Can you tell me what happened?', I was inviting a co-authored version that focused on eventual safety with her boyfriend, leaving other possible events unacknowledged.

Twenty-three years have elapsed since I heard those responses, years in which the term 'incest' has been replaced with the expression 'sexual abuse'. But this was 1979 and, although I was prepared for some distressing accounts, I was not prepared for this. I was prepared for my respondents' distress but not for my own. Frances explained that I was only the third person she had told about these events. Throughout the interview, and as I left her, she appeared calm. I left her house sobered by the interview, all thought of work rates by now abandoned, and walked up the road to Gillian's.

Fortunately, Gillian had had an uneventful adolescence. At the time of interview, she was seven months' pregnant. The interview was progressing well and she had described the birth of her first child when she signalled the tragic events of her subsequent reproductive history:

Gillian: [. . .] But he was normal, he was OK. And ever since then I've had Caesarians and lost the babies.

So keen was she to alert me to (or warn me about?) the tale of loss that was about to unfold that in this statement she forgot to mention her other surviving child from her sixth pregnancy. Her second and fifth pregnancies ended in the birth of babies who died at 12 hours and 3 days, respectively. Her third and fourth pregnancies miscarried. She described collapsing at the funeral of her second baby and her inability to visit the grave of the child of her fifth pregnancy until her next pregnancy was confirmed. In addition, she had been unable to conceive at a difficult stage in her first marriage, which ended following the pregnancy of her husband's girlfriend, and her second husband had been embittered by her initial grief response to the second child's death.

Like Frances, Gillian did not appear to be experiencing distress by being asked questions about her history. Early in the interview, she offered to produce her antenatal cards to confirm the dates of pregnancies. I had declined, thinking this might make the recounting a more distressing process. Embedded in her interview was an account of how she had survived psychologically:

Gillian: Well, by the second [miscarriage] I was getting in a pretty bad state, I was on valium and sleeping tablets, I had to avoid mothers with prams [. . .] I got to the stage where I thought, 'Well, this isn't going to beat me!' And I think after I lost the [baby of the second pregnancy] I think if I hadn't've pulled myself together for the sake of the family . . . I got to the stage two or three weeks later when I said, 'Look, Gillian, you've got to pull yourself together or you're going to have a complete breakdown', and looking back I realize that was the turning point and I started to be thankful I had.

As we advanced through her tragic reproductive history, the impact on myself of booking interviews so close together was beginning to become clear. The transcript indicates that I seemed to respond with sympathy but my memory of the experience of that interview was of running out of ways to say, 'How did you feel at that time?', and that, when transcribing it, my voice went lower and lower as the interview progressed. In addition, concern with time was beginning to surface again. I had booked another interview soon after the hour would be up with Gillian, and was caught between the need to give proper space and time to her unfolding complex history, and possible problems of arriving late for the third interview. I was already resolving to space interviews more carefully, to try to resolve the incompatibility of 'getting the research done', the ethics of in-depth interviewing, and the emotional impact on me as the researcher.

The third interview, with Gina, which I made just in time, I recall as comparatively uneventful. Looking back at the transcript, it is clear that by this stage in the morning's work I was not following up issues that might, in other circumstances, have prompted further questions.

I returned home to a large college house shared with other women students, who were all supportive of my work and often made sympathetic enquiries about how the interviews were progressing. On that day, I indicated that the content of the interviews had been distressing but that I could not talk about this for reasons of confidentiality. Looking back, of course, it was anonymity that was crucial as I would later quote from the interview data in writing up the thesis. As it was, my housemates respected the boundaries I (mis)placed around my work and I reflected alone on its content. At my next supervision my supervisor was sympathetic, though, as I recall, we did not discuss my feelings for long. At that time, there was little tradition of support for the researcher's emotions, but rather a concentration on what the interviewing process might mean for the respondent and the importance of responding appropriately to any distress that might be observed. Understanding disadvantage and suffering was the sociologist's chosen lot, and, to mix the metaphor thoroughly, if you couldn't stand the heat you should get out of the kitchen.

So what did I learn that fateful morning? Aside from spacing interviews to allow them to run over time if the respondent wished, and to allow time for myself to recover from the intensity of the exchange, other points emerged. I realized that there are no 'safe' questions. Any enquiry may produce an unexpected response, and the unexpectedness may be on the part of the researcher rather than the respondent. In addition to the problems of 'stirring things up' for the respondent, the researcher may end up shocked, distressed or disturbed by the account produced. I should say that none of the disclosures of my respondents had personal resonance with my own life, but presumably this has happened to other researchers. The ability to deal with the emotional heat in the kitchen is also clearly historically situated. Researchers undertaking a similar study today would come to that work with a clearer understanding of the nature and prevalence of what we now call sexual abuse, and would be more familiar with issues of pregnancy loss, if not on the scale of Gillian's experience.

Many years and several interview studies later, I am aware that even experienced researchers will encounter situations that may take them by surprise, that research may be hard labour and that the co-authoring process of interviewing may cast emotional shadows that reach well beyond the temporal confines of the research project.

The idea that it is not always possible to second-guess how others may react to our research questions is also central to Emma Williamson's vignette. In her doctoral study of domestic violence, she conducted interviews with women who had experienced violence and the health professionals who cared for them. Whilst Williamson correctly anticipated that the interviews would cause the women (and herself) some distress, she was somewhat thrown when her line of questioning also upset one of the health-care professionals she interviewed. Like Thomas, Williamson concludes there are no 'safe' questions and, perhaps more importantly, no 'safe' research participants.

Research, tears and audio-tape

Emma Williamson

My doctoral research involved talking to two seemingly distinct groups of participants: women who had experienced domestic violence and health-care professionals. Even before I began my interviews with the women, I was well aware that I would be asking them to recall very personal and traumatic experiences. Consequently, I spent a long time justifying to myself the need to put them in potentially difficult and distressing situations. The only way I felt able to do this was to ensure that the research would be 'useful' to people other than myself. I was also a little concerned that I was not a trained counsellor, yet the interview process can, on occasion, mimic a therapeutic situation.

My first interview was certainly a baptism by fire. It involved a woman who had lived for 23 years in an extremely abusive relationship. She was clearly anxious about the interview, making it clear what she did not want me to tape-record it. Before I had a chance to get some paper and a pen out of my bag (so I could take written notes instead) she had literally launched into her story. Throughout the interview, she had an unnerving habit of regularly inserting my name into her sentences as a way of ensuring that I was engaging fully with her experiences. I found her anxieties extremely difficult to deal with.

On another occasion, I was interviewing a woman who initially appeared very self-confident. During the course of the interview she started to cry, and, as was my usual practice, I asked her if she would like me to stop the tape. 'No I wouldn't', she responded. I tried to calm her down by saying 'this is not a test', to which she replied 'this is my test'. I felt very helpless. She seemed clear that she did not want to stop the interview, whilst I on the other hand was less sure about proceeding, given the amount of distress it was causing her. Incidents such as these forced me to think of things that I could do to avoid feeling similarly powerless and upset in the future. This included accessing counselling services at the University in order to de-brief, taking time off between interviews to unwind, and re-joining a circus skills group. My juggling certainly improved during the remainder of my fieldwork!

Whilst I had expected my interviews with the women to be upsetting (for them and for me), I had been much more complacent about my interviews with health professionals, and this was not always justified. During an interview with a practice nurse about domestic violence, I was taken by surprise when she became distressed. Rather than recounting her professional dealings with domestic violence as I had expected, my interview prompted her to recall her personal experiences of attempting to deal with domestic violence within her own family network. I learned a powerful lesson from this interview: you cannot always predict who will get distressed and who will not. Researchers need to be prepared for a whole range of emotional responses from a whole range of research participants.

Thomas's (and to a lesser extent Williamson's) vignette draws attention to the ways in which research can have an emotional impact not only on our research participants, but also upon ourselves. This issue is also movingly illustrated by Catherine Exley, who undertook qualitative research with people who were dying and/or bereaved. In sharing her emotional reactions at various points during her study – which included anger, distress and profound sadness – Exley highlights an ambiguity that may characterize the relationship between ourselves and our research participants (see also Chapter 3). As a researcher, she felt she did not have the 'right' to grieve for research participants who died, although this did not stop her from doing so. Likewise, whilst she never really became a 'friend' to the people she interviewed, she felt that by trying to empathize with their experiences, she lost the protective 'buffer' of being an objective 'stranger' who was emotionally distanced from their lives.

Emotional fact

Catherine Exley

Fact: Conducting research is hard work. Fact: Research takes up an awful lot of time. Fact: Research will often take over your life for a prolonged period of time. Fact: The research world can be a very lonely place. Fact: Research requires an awful lot of emotional energy and many emotions from the researcher. Fact: People seem to forget to tell you this when you embark on your first piece of research.

My particular area of research is generally met with a range of responses from mere curiosity to outright revulsion – after all, why should anyone want to do research with people who are dying or bereaved? There must be something slightly 'odd' about me. Perhaps working with such groups of people brings with it its own particular research dilemmas, but I suspect many of the experiences I have encountered over the last few years are not peculiar to research on dying and death.

During the course of various studies, like many other qualitative researchers, I have spent many hours sitting in people's homes listening to their stories, talking about their lives and answering their questions. Often I have just sat and listened, occasionally asking another question. I have sat as people have laughed, and I have waited as people have cried. There have been many occasions during which silence has been hard to bear. I have sat and waited for someone to get through a moment when they have been unable to speak, because it was important for them to make a particular point. Learning to accept respondents' emotions and do nothing remains, for me, one of the hardest parts of research.

At times, I have had to keep my own emotional responses in check, when I have heard something that has made me angry or has been extremely distressing. I have listened to personal and political views I did not agree with, and managed (I hope) to keep my own views private. I have listened as people with whom I found some kind of connection – my own age, my mother's age, the same laugh as my friend – talked about their hopes for and fears about their own dying and death, and I have fought back the tears. I have sat and listened while a young woman with advanced cancer talked about managing her morphine dosage so that she could ensure her two young sons were in from playing out in the street, and how the children then put themselves to bed when she fell asleep. To her this was nothing extraordinary. Nor indeed did she express any overt anger when she described how she needed to keep her handbag with her at all times because her partner had a drug habit and was stealing her morphine tablets from her; she remained calm. I raged somewhere deep inside.

After conducting interviews, I have taken the tapes home and spent many hours and days transcribing them. In one project in which I interviewed people who were dying, as time progressed it became increasingly difficult to deal with both respondents' emotions and my own. Doing this kind of research for a prolonged period of time certainly has its effects. There have been many occasions when I have been unable to face listening to another interview. However, managing and dealing with one's own emotions and emotional reactions isn't just confined to the fieldwork process. Sitting alone reading and re-reading transcripts can be emotionally draining. In my case, I still find that reading the words of people who are now dead can provoke grief and sadness as I remember and reflect.

When people have died, as many have, I have experienced many different emotions. Not surprisingly (although it is hard to say this) some people's deaths had little or no effect on me. The reality is that during fieldwork, as in life, you're likely to develop a greater rapport with some people than others. In everyday life that's fine, but for me at times it has been difficult to accept. Surely I *should* feel something? At the opposite end, I have felt (and sometimes continue to feel) a profound sense of loss when some people whom I have interviewed have died. Again, this is difficult to reconcile with the reality of my relationship with them. I have at most only met these people three times, and while it is true that they have shared some very personal experiences and thoughts with me, I have no 'right' to grieve. Indeed, those people whose deaths have had a profound effect on me would probably be surprised – after all, I was just an interviewer with a tape recorder, why would I feel anything when they died? I had no long-term, or recognized, relationship with them. They didn't love me, and I didn't love them. Of course, all this is true, but when one respondent, of whom I was particularly fond, died before I went away on holiday (in the UK), I found myself calling to check my voicemail every couple of days to find out when her funeral would be, and I had every intention of cutting my holiday short if that was necessary (ultimately it wasn't). Extreme? Maybe. Mad? Probably. Honest? Yes. I will never forget that baking hot September day when mourners gathered in floating cotton summer dresses, I still can't hear either that Soft Cell song or that obscure Led Zeppelin tune without recalling that day.

Not all research involves this kind of emotion, but it will no doubt bring with it its own emotional challenges. When spending any prolonged period of time in a research environment we need to be aware that it is likely to have some effect on our own lives. I have laughed and cried, alone and with others. I have raged at the injustice of illness and the inequity in society. It really is not an overstatement to say that there are people I have interviewed who will remain with me always. I can still see their faces and remember their words. Conducting research has taught me a great deal about human nature, human relationships and also about myself. Fact: I never knew any of this when I started out.

One particularly important message we should take from Exley's vignette is that our research may continue to have an emotional effect upon us long after we have finished gathering our data. As Exley has demonstrated, revisiting our data for the purposes of transcription, analysis and writing up may also involve us revisiting and re-experiencing emotions, or, indeed, encountering new ones.

That research may have long-lasting emotional effects on us is also highlighted and discussed by Claire Foster, who reflects upon the research she undertook with young people with cystic fibrosis (a life-threatening genetic disease). Foster was profoundly moved by the stories she heard during her interviews and also by the warmth, hospitality and trust that study participants bestowed on her. For her, emotional detachment often proved impossible, and thus 'letting go' at the end of the study was not an easy or straightforward process.

Loosening the bond

Claire Foster

Several years ago, I conducted an interview study involving young people with cystic fibrosis[2] (CF), their siblings and parents. I had worked with young people before, but it was the first time I had interviewed people with a life-threatening condition. The interviews explored coping with intensive daily treatment, growing up with CF, and the impact of the illness on the family. Some interviewees were very well at the time of the interview, while others were experiencing deteriorating health and increasing disability. I was a 26-year-old postgraduate student travelling the length and breadth of Devon and Cornwall to visit families in their homes, sampling tea and cakes *en route*.

I had completed a ten-week interviewing skills course, in which I learned to avoid leading questions and practised open-ended questions (which elicited fascinating facts about fellow students' clog-dancing hobbies) whilst trying to keep a straight face – not always successfully. Nevertheless, at the beginning of the project, armed with my new skills, I was still very much feeling my way into interviewing 'real people' about serious issues. I was extremely nervous about the types of questions I was proposing to ask. In particular, I felt worried that my questions might upset interviewees, uncertain about my right to provoke this upset, and unsure how I would react to tears and distress. I had not really thought about how I would feel once the interview was over.

One of my first interviews was with an 18-year-old woman whom I shall call Izzy. It was a glorious summer's day and I had got up to my usual route-finding antics in the car trying to locate her house. After untangling myself from my map and putting away my compass and GPS device, I took a couple of minutes to focus on the interview and think about the questions I wanted to ask. There was a moment of trepidation as I stood on the doorstep: Would she be happy to speak to me? Would we get on? Would she raise issues that I felt uncomfortable with? Would I look nervous? Should I have eaten those raw onions? I rang the doorbell and was greeted by an attractive, vivacious, and extremely likeable young woman who immediately made me feel at ease.

Izzy talked and talked and talked and was so full of life and upbeat that it was impossible not to warm to her. She had recently spent two weeks in hospital due to a chest infection (a complication of CF). She was excited about going on holiday with friends to Spain the next day to let her hair down and enjoy the sun, sea and sand. It would be the first time that she had been abroad without her family, and she was pleased to escape reminders of hospital and treatment. Her enthusiasm was contagious, and we chatted and laughed about holidays and favourite destinations. She was not obviously upset by any of my questions and talked openly about her future plans, such as getting married and having a family, shadowed by the prospect of her early death. She also confided that she was often 'slack' in doing her treatment.[3] She found it very intrusive and it reminded her of the illness she wanted to forget. I felt a great deal of sympathy for her as a young person struggling to lead a 'normal' life while having to manage an extremely demanding illness. I could not advise or encourage her to do her treatment and did not want to come across as patronizing or judgemental.

I found the interview a very positive and humbling experience and was impressed by Izzy's strength in dealing with CF. However, when I left the house it dawned on me that, unlike me, this vibrant 18-year-old was unlikely to see her 26th birthday. I felt extremely sorry for both her and her family, who were being robbed of a future together. I felt a sense of helplessness and frustration. What was the point of my research project? Was it really going to make any difference? During the interview, I had tried to adhere to the things I had learned during my interviewing course. I did not feel that the interview itself had gone badly, but felt frustrated that, as a researcher, I could not offer any advice or help to Izzy and her family. I had collected the data I needed and would spend a year or so collecting more. Then I would analyse it, before writing it up and publishing it. It all felt so abstract and I wanted to be able to do something more immediate and useful. I was unprepared for the emotional roller coaster I found myself on, which made me question the entire purpose of the research.

Despite my concerns that my project was too abstract, it became clear after a while that the families were grateful that someone was taking an interest in them and listening to their stories. This taught me that the interviews themselves could be a positive experience, not only for me but also for those taking part. I also kept in regular contact with the health professionals in the CF clinic (from which interviewees were recruited) and updated them on the study's progress. Maintaining this contact gave me a sense that the research was having some direct impact.

Often I would spend several hours in a family home with several members of the family and very quickly established a bond with them, perhaps due to the fact that I was a stranger interested in them or because I warmed to their pets. I was introduced to the family cats, dogs, and once had to deal with a runaway hamster. All part of the interview experience. Despite this relatively short contact with the young people and their families, I had to resist the temptation to become overly involved, and at times I found it difficult to 'let go'. It is essential to ensure that you have adequate support for yourself and also to reflect upon how your interaction with interviewees may have a similar effect on them. I did not always take the opportunity to talk through the interviews with my supervisor, but I would certainly recommend this to anyone embarking on a project with vulnerable groups, or which involves discussing sensitive issues.

Although the initial interviews can feel quite raw, you do learn to deal with the emotional aspects and learn strategies for coping with emotionally laden interactions. Whilst interviewing people with CF could be difficult and could churn up all sorts of negative emotions (both in interviewees and in myself), overall it was an extremely rewarding and emotionally enriching experience. Interviewees demonstrated enormous strength in coping with CF. I was greatly touched by their stories.

Whilst I was writing up my thesis I was concerned that I would appear patronizing. Izzy was 'sitting on my shoulder' in those endless and at times lonely hours, keeping tabs on the tone of my writing. I know the end product was by no means perfect, but it was extremely helpful to keep real people in mind when writing. Some years later, I still think about the people who took part in my study and I wonder how they are all getting on.

Whilst Exley and Foster describe some of the difficulties we may experience when trying to disengage from our research, Sue Cox questions whether disengagement should always and necessarily be our goal. She reflects on 'a small but pivotal moment' in her research with people who had Huntington's disease, which led her to re-evaluate her own values and world-view, and to conclude that living life more impulsively can (sometimes) be a good thing. Thus, as Cox suggests, research encounters may change us forever (hopefully for the better) and should be acknowledged and cherished accordingly.

Graceful (dis)engagement: reflections on 'exiting' the field

Sue Cox

I: Point of entry

My partner and I are vacationing at one of the warmest lakes in western Canada. The late August sun is hot and the breeze balmy. The water is sparkling, beckoning, as blue as blue can be. I hesitate before diving in, remembering a man I knew who plunged, joyfully, into a much colder lake than this. My memory of him is clear, the details of the moment etched forever in my mind's eye.

Choosing a pseudonym for this man requires reflection. I cannot use his real name for reasons of confidentiality, and yet it feels disrespectful, even though it is now many years later, not to choose a name that has lasting personal significance. I have been changed by knowing him or perhaps by having the experience of trying to sum up what knowing him now means to me.

My habit of asking research participants to affirm my choice of a pseudonym is not an option and I eventually decide to call this man David. I have a brother named David and he has many of the same virtues as the man I knew, the man who plunged into the lake. The name David also resonates for me with a sense of faith and purpose as well as perseverance.

David was one of those people who teach you something so profound, so elemental, that you need time to let life encircle it, time to feel how it guides you in who you are and how you see the world. This kind of understanding is one of the greatest rewards of doing qualitative research, but it is not something that you can go looking for. Sometimes you are extremely fortunate in that someone says or does something that takes you into their world, lets you glimpse what is beneath the surface. Though you may not know it at the time, the experience nudges something deep inside you. Looking back, you realize that you are different because of this experience.

II: The moment

I met David almost ten years ago when I was a volunteer staff person at a week-long retreat for people with Huntington's disease (HD).[4] The experience of volunteering at the retreat was not officially part of my research on the social and familial implications of predictive testing for HD, but it was integral to being able to do that research in a more meaningful way. Being at the retreat allowed me to discover how to be a researcher and friend to people with HD. It taught me to be open and to trust, to receive care as well as to offer it.

On the day in question, the day that David plunged into the lake, we (that is everyone at the Huntington's retreat) had gone on a field trip to a nearby park. We always went to the same place as the terrain was reasonably level and most people with HD could manage a leisurely walk around the lake without risking a fall. There were also lots picnic tables for us to spread out our copious picnic fare.

It was an unusually hot day for mid-May and the cloudless sky was cause for celebration as rain had, in other years, forced us to stand under the cedar trees eating soggy sandwiches for lunch. We all piled into the yellow school bus we had chartered for the trip. The driver loaded our supplies through the emergency exit at the rear of the bus. Everyone had been instructed to bring a hat and to wear sensible shoes. The camp nurse packed extra sunscreen. The retreat co-ordinator did a head count (26), and we were off.

The bus ride to the lake did not take very long, maybe half an hour, but it was long enough for those on the sunny side of the bus to become warm and sweaty. Not all of the windows opened properly and the still thickness of the air made us wilt. When we arrived at our appointed spot near the lake, David was among the first to disembark from the bus. Baseball cap turned at a rakish angle, he made a beeline for the sparkling blue water.

David was a big man and it wasn't easy to match his stride. Leaving a trail of hastily discarded clothes, a knapsack, sunglasses and shoes behind him, he hit the beach area almost at a run. There was no stopping him. With only his shorts remaining, David plunged into the water, completely submersing himself in its coolness. A moment later, he resurfaced smiling and laughing, his joy in the moment undiluted by the anxiety that briefly gripped each of us staff persons – 'What if he didn't resurface?'

David was sometimes impatient. If he wanted to do something, he wanted to do it now. He did not want to hear why he should wait. This was more than David's 20-something enthusiasm, it was part of the way that HD affected him.

In the literature on HD, the inability to delay gratification or to refrain from socially unacceptable behaviour is sometimes referred to as an 'impulse-control' problem. I don't know about this way of looking at it. Too much patience sometimes stops us from living as fully as we should.

III: Re-entry

When David died from HD in the autumn of this year, family, friends and members of the Huntington's community gathered to grieve and to celebrate his life. The church was full and a great many people spoke about David's compassion for others, commitment to social justice and zest for life. There was great sadness but the faith that David was in another more beautiful and peaceful place outshone this sadness.

I respect but do not share in this kind of faith, this belief in an afterlife. It is enough for me to know that people live on in and through the thoughts and feelings, memories and actions of others. Research sometimes helps us sort out our personal feelings about these big questions. Not once and for all, but for now.

Observing what the Huntington's community found most important to grieve and to celebrate in David's life, I learned what I most value and wish to enact within my own life. Looking at the lake, I now feel, with David, that impatience is sometimes a virtue. I feel myself hesitate and then I plunge in.

IV: Reflections

Ethnographic research often requires a long period of engagement within a community or research setting. Long engagement with a community sometimes does, however, make for a difficult period of disengagement when data collection and analysis phases of the research are complete. Research participants have, in some cases, become friends and their daily struggles have engendered new loyalties and commitments. How do we, as researchers, navigate this terrain? What are our responsibilities to our research participants and communities as well as ourselves?

Looking back on my experiences in doing research within the Huntington's community, I realize that it makes little sense to view research as a linear process that is marked by points of entry, immersion and exit from the field. This view is one-dimensional; it neglects the recursiveness of the research process, the rich and varied ways that we experience and re-experience specific moments in time. It allows us to think that once the research results are disseminated we are done with the awkward yet necessary struggle to articulate who we are in relation with those we study.

My story about David focuses on one small but pivotal moment in the research process. This moment reminds me that it is not a method of dis-engagement that I seek when completing a research study. It is a method of renewed engagement, a lasting commitment to acting upon the practical wisdom I have, so graciously, been offered.

So what are the implications of what we have read so far? Arguably, most of the contributors have shared extreme experiences, in so far as conducting (in-depth) research with people who are dying (Exley) and/or have life-threatening conditions (Foster and Cox) is likely to raise particularly emotive issues. Yet, as Exley's vignette serves to highlight, there are various issues which all of us who undertake face-to-face research may encounter, whatever the focus of our research – for example, having to keep our emotional reactions in check when we listen to personal and political views with which we may not agree. We should also keep in mind that even when a research topic (or a particular question raised in an interview) may seem harmless and emotionally uncontentious at the outset, things can prove very different in practice, as Thomas's and Williamson's stories so vividly demonstrate.

In sharing the emotional aspects of their research, the contributors highlight a need (implicitly, if not explicitly) for more formal and informal support to be made available to those who undertake research. Clearly this is a message we should all take on board, whether we are the people who roll up our sleeves and collect and analyse the data or those who commission or supervise research projects. If we (researchers) need emotional support, then we should seek it, and we should not feel embarrassed or ashamed to do so. This support can come in many forms, be it 'off-loading' over a cup of tea (or a strong drink!) with our friends, partner or supervisor or, if necessary, seeking the help of a trained counsellor. At the same time, grant holders, project managers and academic supervisors need to think carefully about the ways in which they can offer emotional support to those undertaking research (see also Hubbard *et al.* 2001; Johnson and Clarke 2003). In some cases, this may require building formal supervision and (counselling) sup-port into a research design. In others, simply making oneself available – for example, being at the end of a phone so a researcher can debrief after an interview – may suffice. Whatever strategies we decide on, it is very import-ant to keep in mind that the emotional aspects of undertaking research may not necessarily stop when a study comes to an end. As the vignettes in this section have illustrated, doing research can change us in permanent ways – hopefully for the better.

Emotions are unpredictable things

As some of the contributors have already highlighted, it can sometimes prove impossible to second-guess how we (and others) will actually feel about the research we undertake. Sometimes we may end up becoming upset – or upsetting others – in ways we simply could not have anticipated. Likewise, on occasions, we may surprise ourselves by coming away from an interview or fieldwork encounter feeling happy and upbeat, despite working on a research topic which we expected to find distressing. Indeed, as Young and Lee (1996) have observed, in many cases there are no hard and fast 'rules for feelings' that we can follow when we undertake research, an issue made very evident in Stefan Timmermans' and Ann Robertson's contributions below. The section concludes with vignettes by Julia Twigg and Sue Cox, who discuss some of the (emotional) strategies they have used when dealing with unpredictable emotional reactions in others, in the absence of more formal rules of conduct.

Autopsy, like death in general, is a taboo subject (Gorer 1965); hence Timmermans expected to find his participant observation research in a US coroner's office an emotionally challenging experience. While this sometimes proved to be the case, Timmermans (much to his own surprise) also found the experience of watching autopsies both fascinating and mesmerizing, a reaction which, as he suggests, other people might have regarded as inappropriate and disrespectful (and hence which stopped him from sharing his emotions with them). Thus, for Timmermans, watching autopsies really was a conversation stopper, but not necessarily for the reasons we might assume.

How can you watch autopsies?

Stefan Timmermans

My research is a conversation stopper. When I mention that I observe medical examiners – the American equivalent of coroners – listeners have a slightly alarmed look in their eyes and I can almost sense their search for a different topic. But first the inevitable question comes. With incredulity in their eyes, they ask, 'How can you stand watching dead bodies and autopsies?' The corpses in the medical examiner's office indeed do not look pretty: they are often mutilated due to various forms of trauma, or they are in an advanced state of decomposition after being holed up in a sweltering summer apartment for a couple of days. Wildlife gets to the body before the medical examiner's staff: rats, ants, cockroaches, maggots, and occasionally even lobsters when the corpse is dragged out of the ocean. Sometimes the corpse looks pristine, like the suntanned body of a 7-year-old girl swept away in the surf. I wonder why she is not moving. The good-looking corpses inevitably remind me of what could have been. If the girl's parents had not been busy setting up the beach parasol, maybe she would not have been swept from her surfboard. But the fact that she is in a morgue makes the question moot. All cases, even the babies, are dead. It's a given. Yet, I discovered that it is not difficult to watch corpses if you learn to look and feel from a professional perspective.

I remember my first autopsy: a middle-aged man who might have died naturally from cancer or helped the dying process along and overdosed on pain medication. It took me more than nine months to negotiate access to observing autopsies, and I wanted to make sure that I 'acted appropriately', that is, did not faint or became nauseous. When the pathologist's scalpel made the Y-shaped incision in the chest of the corpse, slowly peeled away the skin and cut through the rib cage with a bone saw, I felt a mood shift: anxiety gave way to curiosity. What would we find in this bundle of organs? The Greek etymological roots of autopsy refer to seeing for oneself. Autopsying relies on gross anatomy, and gross does not mean disgusting, but observable by the eye. Guided by the pathologist's clues and directions of what to look for, I felt a sense of fascination and anticipation. The small scalpel incisions on the heart showed that the man had coronary occlusions, adding another possible cause of death. The plot thickened: what killed this person? The pathologist pended the case, his final cause of death would depend on toxicology results. Later, he laughed away both my anticipated anxiety and fascination with the possible cause of death. For him, the case constituted one of the most routine autopsies. When I mentioned how struck I was with the similarity between human and animal organs, he shook his head, and I noted that he ate a meatball sandwich for lunch.

While observing the signs of death was not often taxing, this research was emotionally evocative. One set of emotions resides in the noticeable tenseness when the scene investigator's phone rings. While sitting in the technician's lounge, morgue assistant Zachary explained his unease. 'What if I pick up the phone,' he said, 'and the hospital spells the name of the deceased as first name G-R-A-C-E, last name J-O-H-N-S-O-N?' He had spelled his wife's name. He explained: 'You never know who the call will be about. I have been living my entire life in this area and sooner or later we might bring in someone I know.' Driving back home later that day, I also started to wonder. What if a car hit me and I died? Who would do my autopsy? The office had recently done a case of a toddler who died when running into traffic. I worried about my own 2-year-old daughter. Actually while assisting in that particular autopsy, Zachary had told me that he was going to give his kids a big hug when he came home.

Stories of people dying suddenly are common in newspapers, but the difference of conducting research in the medical examiner's office is the possible proximity of the deaths. Observing the autopsy, I cannot glance over the item in the morning paper but am forced to notice how the accident unfolded: the mother who was momentarily distracted by a neighbour, the toddler wandered into the street, screeching brakes, ambulance, CT scan, intensive care, declining vital parameters, comfort care, and death. Then I see the child when the assistant opens the body-bag: a small girl wrapped up in a protective collar, IV lines, disinfectant swabs, tracheal tube . . . I did not meet the parents but it is not difficult to imagine their deep grief. The pathologist cuts the body, not to detect a cause of death but to verify the lethality of the damage. In those cases, I try to keep a distance, walk between autopsies, try not to linger – visually and mentally.

While medical examiners make forensic sense of these deaths, there remains something intrinsically unexplainable; something residual that is too idiosyncratic, yet all too common in suspicious deaths. Every morning meeting in the medical examiner's office I listen to the variations. A 41-year-old woman drives home from her aunt's funeral, deeply distraught. Her husband urges her to put on her seatbelt and let him drive. She slips off the road, overreacts, yanks the steering wheel, the car bounces against some trees, and she hits her head against the car frame. The car is fine except for some chipped paint and a flat tyre. She is dead, fatal brain injuries. How does one prevent such a freak occurrence? What lessons do I take from that situation? How does that reflect on the mortality of my loved ones and myself?

These emotions of uncertainty and realizations of the frailty of life call out for a discussion with others. But the question 'How can you watch autopsies?' serves as a conversation stopper. The question suggests that only the presumed gruesome aspects of this research can be discussed or affirmed. The other emotional turmoil (and fascination) about mortality should not be brought up, unless I risk making listeners very uncomfortable. Forensic pathologists work in a world where death is dirty. Cutting up bodies, even with a medico-legal mandate, does not fit with a sanitized approach towards death. While it is fascinating to see the homicide victim that everyone reads about in the morning paper, I quickly learned to keep quiet about it. I don't discuss my research with my colleagues. Not because I want to protect confidentiality per se, but because being comfortable among *those* deaths is unacceptable. The stigma of death rubs off on the pathologists and on me. In my opinion, the stigmatization is really the source of emotional distress, not the visual display of a corpse. We are all implicated in those emotions, and doing research in a morgue does not only confirm stigmas but magnifies how I am looking for reassurance in light of mortality.

Robertson, like Timmermans, also found that the emotions she experienced during her research were not necessarily those she had anticipated at the outset. Far from finding her research with women who had a high risk of developing breast cancer upsetting and emotionally isolating, Robertson often found herself overtaken by an overwhelming sense of curiosity. Her experiences serve to demonstrate that even research that explores potentially distressing subjects can be full of fun and laughter, not just tears. Furthermore, Robertson's account shows that we enter our research, and engage with our research participants, not as disembodied, emotionally detached researchers, but as embodied, sentient and sensual beings (see Coffey 1999).

Bawdy tales: talking to women about their breasts

Ann Robertson

I have spent a lot of time in the last few years talking to women about their breasts. The actual focus of my research has been on women's perceptions of risk for breast cancer, but what we – my study participants and I – have generally ended up spending most of our time talking about is these particular body parts that make us and mark us, unequivocally, as women.

I came upon this particular research area by what, in hindsight, appears to be a very 'unscientific' conflation of events, which may be, in the end, the way most of us come to our research. The first was a photograph on the cover of the *New York Times Magazine* of a woman wearing a dress that had been especially designed to reveal her naked right chest. There it was – her right breast – gone! And, in its place, a long, brutal mastectomy scar. I sat and looked at that photograph for days, feeling a mixture of horror, admiration, pity, fascination and, ultimately, curiosity. What was going on here? How was it that this photo could be published? How were we to 'read' this image?

The second event was my visit to an art exhibition by breast cancer survivors, which included photographs, sculpture, fabric art and painting. But the particular display that caught my attention was a 3–4 minute video loop of women's breasts – young, old, large, small, black, white, pert, droopy – in various activities – bathing, during a breast self-exam, receiving a clinical breast exam, revealing a mastectomy scar, and so on. What struck me was that there was not one image that showed a woman's breasts in an erotic, sensual or sexual context. And, again, I wondered 'what is going on here?' Mainly, I wondered if the intensity of the breast cancer message had so intensified women's fears about breast cancer that they had lost all sense of their breasts as sensual, sexual, erotic. And that was when I decided to investigate the nature and extent of women's perceptions of risk for breast cancer.

So, what is it like to sit with women for an hour or more and talk about breasts – theirs, mine, breasts in general? In the course of conducting individual interviews and focus groups, I was often struck by the shared shyness, humour, self-effacement and sheer raunchiness that we women (interviewer and interviewee alike) experienced and expressed when talking about breasts. These shared feelings were revealed not only by what was said, but also by gestures, laughter, tears, tone of voice, glances and eye contact (or the lack of), and by what was not said. They were also revealed by my own visual, verbal and bodily responses.

In the course of these discussions, many women joked and laughed, some-times self-effacingly, about being 'too flat' or 'too big' or 'droopy'. I would join in with the laughter – raising an eyebrow, smiling wryly – indicating that I, too, shared the near-universal concern about the 'okay-ness' of our female bodies.

Ivy: They get in the way, they prevent me from seeing my toes unless I lean back (laughter).
Me: Well, they're certainly the most visible sign of our being a woman.
Ivy: Yeah (laughs). Especially when you can see them coming around corners.

Many times and at odd moments, conducting these interviews didn't feel like research – it often felt more like sitting and talking with a woman friend over coffee or lunch. On several occasions, I had flashes of being 11 or 12, talking and giggling with a girl friend about our delight and the agony of buying our first bra, whether or not to buy 'falsies' and stuff the mostly empty cups with our socks. And we would relive the embarrassment of going out in public with these things that protruded from our chests and what that meant about what we were becoming.

It was impossible not to take note of the actual physical presence of the women's – and my – breasts. As they talked, many of them glanced down at their own breasts, gestured towards them, cupped them, patted them – one woman even went so far as to give her breasts separate names – Sue and Gail! I have often wondered what the professional transcriber made of the gales of laughter that followed that one! It was not possible for me not to look at the participants' breasts on such occasions. And I found myself responding in kind, glancing at, touching, pointing towards my own breasts as we went through the questions on my Interview Guide. It was almost as if we were in a kind of gestural conversation that went alongside the words we were speaking.

Of course, the interviews were not always sprinkled with laughter. Some women's mothers had died of breast cancer and when they talked about this their eyes would fill with tears and sometimes they would cry.

Elaine: When my mother first got breast cancer, I was in sixth grade . . . I was the oldest child and at that time I didn't know anything; I remember my father saying to me, 'you know, your mother had one of her breasts removed' and I remember saying 'will it grow back', you know, what do you know as an 11- or 12-year-old kid. And he said, 'no, no it won't'. And I remember him saying, 'Don't tell any of your friends', you know, like she doesn't want anybody to know about it . . . And my father told me later at the time the doctors told him that she had a 5 per cent chance of living the next five years. Because she'd had it spread to the lymph nodes and stuff. And they didn't tell HER [angrily]. I found this out much later, you know, much later, not at the time.
Me: That must have been really hard for you.
Elaine: When I think about breast cancer, I think for me it's more what breast

cancer has taken away, and the fact that it's left me as a motherless daughter [angrily]. That I think is mostly what I live with.

Throughout Elaine's account, it was impossible for me not to feel her 12-year-old confusion and fear and her ever-present grief at the loss of her mother. I felt my own eyes well up with tears. Oddly enough, I did not feel uncomfortable with this; the tears and the sadness – hers and mine – felt like a very real and natural accompaniment to what Elaine was talking about.

When I talk to people about my research, they often think that it must be pretty grim and depressing. But I am always struck with how, for the most part, this is not the case. And that makes me wonder, what do I feel as I am conducting these interviews? And I realize that mostly it is curiosity. And I also feel a deep interest in these women as I listen to their stories about these body parts that are so symbolic of what it means to be a woman. And that makes me realize that I like doing this kind of research, in large part, because I like this kind of empathetic conversation with women. And this makes me reflect on what this experience has taught me – as a qualitative researcher – in relation to Bourdieu's injunction 'to attend' and his notion of this kind of research as a kind of intellectual love.

As we have seen, some of the women in Robertson's study did become upset during their interviews. Interestingly, rather than seeing their tears as an indication that she should stop the interview, Robertson considered them to be a natural and inevitable accompaniment to the stories the women were telling, a judgement which, as she suggests, was based on the fact that *she* felt comfortable. But how do we really know when it is time to pull in the reins and to stop an interview (or a particular line of questioning)? Likewise, how far can we, or should we, go in pursuing a line of investigation in order to get the data we think we want? And what should we do if, or when, we realize we have already pushed things too far?

Cox, in her second contribution to this chapter, found it necessary to raise and reflect on these kinds of questions during (and after) an interview she conducted for her study of family members' views of predictive genetic testing for Huntington's disease (HD). She describes how she failed to pick up on the verbal and non-verbal cues her study participant was sending out, cues that signalled her discomfort with some of the questions Cox was asking. This resulted in a very awkward and upsetting situation for both. Hindsight, as Cox concludes, can be a wonderful thing, particularly if we are willing to learn from our mistakes. One lesson Cox shares with us is that if we are in any doubt about what to ask during an interview, or how hard to push things, then we should hold back, for, as she notes, 'people will tell you what you need to know', but only if we let them.

Context, communication and paradox: on learning not to ask 'overly sensitive' questions

Sue Cox

During my doctoral research, I conducted over one hundred interviews with families in which someone was going through predictive genetic testing for Huntington's disease (HD). I talked with people who were going through the process of testing, both before and after they received their results. I also talked with their partners, adult children, parents, siblings and close friends.

These interviews often focused on topics that were difficult or painful for study participants to talk about. Because I was especially interested in how families communicate about genetic information, I asked interviewees to share their experiences of talking with family or friends about being at risk for HD. I wanted to know when and how they first learned that they were at risk for the disease, whether the family history had been a well-guarded secret or had been openly discussed. I wanted to understand how people decided who they would share their test results with, whether it was difficult to tell some people but not others, and why. I wanted, in short, to do an ethnography of communication about a highly personal and potentially stigmatizing form of information.

Before I began the interviews, I wondered what the experience would be like. Would I ask the 'right' questions? Could I rely on myself to know when and when not to probe? Should I strive to be as neutral as possible, or should I act as if I were a 'friend' as well as a researcher? I thought a lot about such questions; they were with me on the bus as I travelled to and from the University, and they permeated many discussions of research design and ethics. A dog-eared copy of Mishler's *Research Interviewing* became a constant companion. However, my most important lessons were learned from the people with whom I talked on and off the record in interviews, during Huntington Society events and at the Annual Retreat for people with HD.

One woman who I interviewed early on in the research taught me a great deal about the complexity of interviewing and, most centrally, the importance of the researcher learning *not* to ask overly sensitive questions. Marie was in her early 40s when she decided to request predictive testing for HD. Like many other people living at risk for HD, she struggled with day-to-day anxieties about if, and when, she would develop signs of onset. Some of the people I interviewed were able to talk about their HD risk in ostensibly objective terms, which did not seem to fracture the subtle balance they had achieved in their every day existence. Marie was, however, highly attuned to the way that spoken language makes things real and, as a result, she found it very difficult to talk about her awareness of the possibility that she might develop HD.

It was difficult to schedule an interview with Marie. She and her husband lived in a small town about two hours' drive from the University and snowy roads completely pre-empted my first attempt to meet with her. When I finally arrived to do the interview, Marie was home alone. She invited me in, put the kettle on and we chatted about the weather, the ski season and recent wildlife sightings in the area. I sensed that she felt a little anxious about the interview so I tried not to move too quickly with my preliminary questions. She seemed to relax and, though she didn't quite forget about the tape recorder, she began to talk about her recent visit to the genetic counselling clinic. I had met her and her husband at the clinic and observed her pre-test counselling session, so I was already familiar with her family history and reasons for wanting predictive testing.

Marie expressed confidence that she was *not* showing signs of onset of HD. She had asked the neurologist about the results of her recent neurological examination and he had told her that they were within the normal range. Marie's younger brother had, however, begun to show definite signs of onset. He lived nearby, so HD was becoming more of a tangible presence in Marie's life. It was, as her husband Peter later said, 'coming closer than we thought'.

As the interview progressed, Marie told me that 'nothing was spoken about too openly' in her family. This had been the case as long as she could remember. There 'wasn't a lot of information' when the family first learned about HD and no one was certain which family members were affected. Referring to her father and his brothers, Marie explained that they felt that the disease had been inherited through their mother's side. It was, however, almost as if their mother had done something wrong by having HD, something morally wrong, and neither Marie's father nor his brothers had wanted to discuss it.

Marie continued to piece things together somewhat reluctantly when I asked her what else she remembered. She said that when she was much younger, her uncle had had HD and her father had been scared by what he'd seen when he went to visit. He had found his brother strapped down to a table because he was moving uncontrollably.

When I asked Marie when she realized that HD is hereditary and that she might also be at risk, she said that she began thinking about this seriously in her early 30s. This was about the same time that her father had been diagnosed with the disease. Marie said that for a long time there hadn't been 'a strong concern for me having it'.

I pressed Marie to say more by asking if she remembered talking to her brothers and sisters about being at risk for HD. She tentatively replied, 'No I don't/W-We didn't talk much about it'. I then asked 'how about your mother, did she talk to you about it?' Marie answered still more tentatively, her words punctuated with enough silences to make me question what it was that I was asking her to tell me.

Well, it's not the kind of thing [long pause] that/I mean we saw it [pause] whenever we went home/what was happening/but as far as discussing it too much, it wasn't really talked about too much.

It wasn't really talked about *too* much and we were, as I later realized, talking about it *too* much. Still, I continued, 'Did you find yourself thinking about it very much at the time, perhaps when you would go to visit or . . .' Marie was hardly breathing as she said,

> Uhm [pause] Well IT was/IT was THERE [pause] I mean IT was uhm [long pause] I think I just want to get some fresh air right now.

Marie stood up and went outside. She closed the door behind her, firmly, and I sat in silence for what seemed like an eternity. I felt stupid and inept, sitting there in Marie's living room. I had not paid enough attention. I was afraid that I had somehow violated her trust.

When I heard Marie open the door, I took a deep breath and self-consciously switched off the tape recorder, embarrassed that I had not thought to do so sooner. Marie had regained her composure enough to suggest that we have some more tea and then maybe 'just talk'. She blew her nose and asked that I not turn the tape recorder on again. We talked for a while about 'safe' topics such as the log house she and her husband had built. When we finished our tea, I stumbled through my gratitude. She was fine, she assured me, and her husband would be home soon.

I waited until I returned home to listen to the interview. It was all there on tape, the important stuff that I had missed. Playing the tape over and over, like a broken record, the 'it' Marie referred to signified to me everything that could not be put into words – the fear, the endless introspection and the unavoidable always-thereness of HD. 'It' loomed too large and demanded too much. 'It' ruptured the conversation because 'it' made me and Marie acutely aware that I had asked her to put into words that which she had told me 'wasn't really talked about too much'. I had pressed Marie to the edge of what she was willing to say and the moment when Marie refused and/or was unable to say anything more about what her experience of 'it' was like was the moment when I understood, with humility, the space between what is and is not said, what is and is not there, what I could and could *not* ask.

It's a lesson I've never forgotten. Though I sometimes wait a very long time for some interviewees to broach a difficult subject or tackle a topic that I'm interested in hearing about, I no longer feel as if I need, or have the right, to 'probe' further. People will eventually tell you what you need to know and, if they do not, their silence should perhaps speak as loudly as their words.

Julia Twigg, like Sue Cox, describes an encounter during her research that caused both her and her research participant to feel awkward and upset. At the end of an interview conducted during her study of older people and bathing, the research participant (an elderly woman) asked if she could listen to the tape recording of their conversation. Twigg felt very uneasy with this request, but she also felt that she had no choice but to comply with the woman's wishes. Twigg's intuition proved to be correct, as listening to her memories played back on the tape had a catastrophic effect on the woman, leaving Twigg with a moral dilemma she then had to attempt to resolve.

Stealing voices . . . or don't play back the tape

Julia Twigg

Mrs W was small and birdlike, living in a neatly furnished sheltered flat in Coastville, a decayed seaside resort on the south coast of England. In her 80s, she was still mentally alert, though with her bad heart and rheumatic joints, she found it hard to move about and needed help with personal care. That was why she was in my sample, for I was doing a study of people living at home who needed help with bathing and washing.

Bathing was not always an easy subject to get people to talk about. In some ways the topic is so mundane that they could not imagine how someone had come from a university to ask them about it: after all, what is there to say about having a bath? But in other ways it is much too sensitive a matter, too personal, too close to the self and to areas of hurt, loss and exposure, for an easy chat. A major part of the interview thus centred on encouraging people to talk freely about things that they never normally spoke about and to venture into areas that could be embarrassing or painful – though could also be funny.

Not all respondents were good at this. Some felt that they really had nothing to say. Others did not want to say much, did not want to be coaxed down this path. Though such responses were significant in themselves, inevitably the 'best' respondents were those who were happy to talk and able to describe their feelings about receiving such help, often in vivid detail. Mrs W was one of these. She told me all about the processes of negotiating help, the struggles with care workers, the ways they were friends but not friends. It was a good interview.

As is the way, in the course of the interview she told me a bit about herself, how she and her husband-to-be – for they had not met at this stage – had come to Britain in the turmoil of the war. She did not directly say she was Jewish, but the circumstances of her life suggested this. This background was not relevant to my study, so I did not explore it further and set about steering the conversation back to bathing. Mrs W warmed to the subject. It was a good session. I was pleased. She had given me some excellent quotes, as well as new insights to illuminate the themes of the research.

Packing up my things, I noticed her looking at the tape recorder with interest. 'I've not seen one of those before', she said, 'What do all the buttons do? Does it play out as well as take in?' I felt uneasy. I could have lied. I wish I had lied. 'Yes', I admitted reluctantly, 'it does'. 'But not terribly well', I added airily, trying to side step what was coming. 'Oh, I'd love to hear it. I've never heard a tape. I've never heard my own voice'. 'Oh, you won't like it', I said, 'the quality will be so bad', and time is getting on – and 'oh dear, oh dear' I thought. On and on she pressed. 'It would be such a treat. Just a little bit'. So with great reluctance I reversed the tape and pressed PLAY.

Her voice filled the room. I watched as her smile dissolved, replaced by a look of dismay and fear. The section we had hit on was one where she was chatting happily about her deceased husband. There was nothing particularly personal about what she was saying, certainly nothing intimate, but I could see that she was aghast at what she had done. She was terribly upset. The whole event had become a disaster. She had chattered unthinkingly into the machine and now it was going to be taken away with all her thoughts. This terrible false voice speaking about her husband, naming his name, talking about their life together – how could it be hers! What had she done?

I tried to reassure her. 'We all find our voices disturbing . . . your name will be kept confidential . . . I won't mention you husband or any personal details . . . the study is all about other things.' But I could not persuade her. The more we talked, the worse it got. Her anxiety and agitation escalated. Suddenly she seemed much more frail than I had realized. I felt terrible. There was nothing to do but to offer to wipe the tape there and then. We sat in silence as I overlaid the recording. Soon it became clear that this would take forever, so I simply promised to destroy the tape. On the way home I pulled into a lay-by overlooking open fields to the coast, broke open the cassette and reeled into the bin handfuls of shining brown tape.

What are the issues here? Data is a bit like hidden treasure, something that the researcher wants to capture, take away, exult over. That image of a precious possession holds good for the respondent also. It is a cliché of anthropology that 'primitive persons' are fearful of having their photograph taken lest their souls be stolen away in the process. But in fact we all feel something of this in relation to confidences given, lives described. There is a primitive magic at work here, particularly when the confidences have been recorded, turned into objects that can be taken from you, spirited away.

I think this is what Mrs W felt. She had handed over something of herself, and listening to the tape made this terrible fact manifest. Her life, her memories, her thoughts were now enclosed in that little crystal box, to be taken away and replayed in goodness knows what circumstances and before what people. In her case, the sense of fear was exacerbated by terrible memories of the consequences that could flow from the revelation of personal data to official persons. We assume a benign state – by and large – but there are many others whose experiences are wholly different and have had good reasons to be fearful.

I felt very bad about upsetting Mrs W. I wanted to keep the data, to be able to take it back to my room at the university, to reflect upon it, code it, use it as a basis for my writing, but I also felt terrible that she was so distressed. I felt guilty about upsetting her. She had agreed freely to take part. She was not withdrawing consent. She was not demanding that the tape be destroyed. She was just terribly, terribly upset. I had to make a decision. And when it came to it, it was feelings that were the guiding matter, not formal research codes. All true morality is felt morality. It may also be considered, but its roots and its guiding principles are felt. Feelings are both a guide to moral action and a motivator and reinforcer of right conduct. What we feel may not always be right: our feelings can lead us astray. But they are a good basic indication. Feeling bad about an interview is a sign that something is probably wrong.

I think that I did the right thing in destroying the tape, though with some anguish as it contained such good data. The question remains, however, about playing back the tape. I did not want to do this. I still regret doing it, as it led to all the trouble, heartache and – for me – loss. And my advice to fellow researchers remains: don't do it . . . don't play back the tape.

Twigg tried to resolve her dilemma by destroying the tape of the interview. What is particularly salient for us to note here is that in attempting to do the right thing by her research participant, Twigg took her steer from her own feelings. As she has described, *she* felt 'guilty' and 'terribly upset' and it was for this reason that she knew she had to do something to rectify the situation. Twigg is not alone in this regard: Cox and Robertson were similarly guided by their emotions when they attempted to determine where to draw the line in their interviews. Robertson, for example, felt it was appropriate to continue her interviews even after some of her participants became visibly upset because she felt comfortable with their tears. Cox, in contrast, knew she had asked too much of the woman she was interviewing (who also broke down in the interview) because she felt 'stupid', 'inept' and 'afraid'.

Perhaps the single most important lesson we can learn from these contributors is that there are no hard and fast rules for dealing with our own and our research participants' emotions, and there may be no ready-made solutions for when things do go wrong. No matter how many books we may read about how to do research, if we want to do the right thing, ultimately our own emotions and intuitions may be our best, and perhaps only, guide.

The emotional career of a contract researcher: nasty, brutish and short

This chapter ends with a contribution from Rachel Grellier, who has worked as a contract researcher for many years. In contrast to the other contributors to this chapter, the emotions Grellier describes were not generated in interactions with particular research participants, on particular occasions or even during particular projects. Rather, they arose as a direct response to her working conditions. As a contract researcher, Grellier has had to endure frustrating and difficult (some would say unacceptable) conditions, such as having no job security and having to relocate in order to secure the next job. Her vignette serves as a powerful reminder that working as a contract researcher may have gradual but long-lasting emotional effects. Indeed, Grellier (like many other contract researchers known to the editors) describes how she now feels so demoralized and burnt out that she is seriously considering an alternative career.

Burnout: the cost of contract research

Rachel Grellier

I have been a contract researcher for ten years. During this time, I've worked in four different universities on numerous studies. Research contracts tend to last no longer than three years; often they are as short as one year, and the temporary nature of the work means following the money even if that means relocating. At the beginning, constantly changing roles was exciting and challenging, and I loved doing research. After being employed on a number of studies (once funding had been secured), I became involved in preparing proposals and helping to manage projects. This gave added job satisfaction as I was beginning to see research from a broader perspective and be involved in projects from beginning to end. Work was varied, stimulating, largely enjoyable, often challenging and fulfilling from both a personal and professional point of view.

After a while, however, I realized that contract research involves a steep learning curve that quickly plateaus out. Working in. academia means long hours, and doing fieldwork often involves evening and weekend work, travelling long distances, and doing things that are not generally recommended, such as spending time alone in strangers' houses discussing personal, intimate and, sometimes, distressing issues. From a professional perspective, levels of responsibility fluctuate and are seldom clearly defined. Having responsibility for data collection and analysis is a major role often leading to the closest knowledge of the study. However, the contract researcher is frequently, in theory, the most junior member of the research team with the least job security, least input into the management of the project, at the same time as having the heaviest work levels in terms of both doing the research and writing up. The increasingly competitive nature of academic funding exacerbates the insecurity and difficult nature of combining these conflicting roles. Academic salaries in no way reflect those of other public sector workers. For example, since 1981 lecturers' salaries have increased (in real terms) by between 5 and 7 per cent compared to a figure of 44 per cent for full-time employees as a whole.[5] In addition, recent figures show that 50 per cent of women academic and research staff are on fixed-term contracts, compared with 38 per cent of men; and almost 50 per cent of non-white British academics are on temporary contracts, compared to 34 per cent of white academics.[6] Recently proposed guidelines to give employees on fixed-term contracts better employment rights are appearing to have the consequences of reducing employment opportunities and forcing relocation on individuals as universities try to avoid redundancy payments to staff who have been on temporary contracts for four years or more. It seems ironic that a sector that has traditionally challenged race, class and gender discrimination, and criticized the costs of economic and employment uncertainty, is now reinforcing this system.

The reality of research is that it seldom begins and ends on the specified contract dates. Preparing a research proposal can take months, while writing, submitting and revising papers is also a protracted process. This means researchers are frequently writing up previous studies while beginning work on a new study. Grant proposals also need to be written to ensure that you'll still be employed when the current project comes to an end. In other words, it's seldom the case of only focusing on one piece of research at a time. Working at weekends and evenings, even when not doing fieldwork, is standard practice for researchers. The funding body paying for your current employment is hardly going to be happy if you only work four days a week because you are busy preparing a proposal or writing up completed research funded by someone else. Admittedly the rewards are publications and further work, but this comes at a cost. For me, the continuous cycle of conducting literature reviews, fieldwork and writing up is no longer a challenge. This is coupled with the constant awareness that there may not be another contract to go on to, as the majority of grant applications are unsuccessful.

My enthusiasm and willingness to accept these working conditions has gradually but inexorably diminished. It's when I see new colleagues excitedly embracing the culture of contract research that I realize that's what I used to be like. Now I am aware of the impact that long-term economic and professional instability has had on me. Looking for yet another job is no longer exciting; trying to finish one project while starting another has more costs than benefits; wondering if there will even be another project is not something that intrigues me – paying a mortgage single-handedly tends to reduce my willingness to take that kind of risk.

The sad thing is that it's not really research itself that I'm disenchanted with: it is more the organization and funding of higher education and research. While research itself is still interesting, this is no longer sufficient, nor is the continual cost that accompanies the effort to remain desirable in terms of future employment. A career in academia seldom leads to fame or fortune but (as we are repeatedly told) has compensations such as flexible working hours, intellectual stimulation and a sense of social worth. After ten years of accepting this, I find that the features which were supposed to compensate for the lack of pay, career structure and security have instead left me burnt out, weary and disillusioned with the system.

For the majority of us who want a career in academic research rather than in teaching, contract research will be our only option. However, before deciding to embark on such a career, we need to be aware that whilst individual research projects may be very rewarding, intellectually challenging and emotionally fulfilling, the conditions in which the work is undertaken may not be quite so acceptable (see also Cunningham-Burley and Backett-Milburn, Chapter 4).

Research work: emotional work

Most of the time doing research is a pleasurable and intellectually rewarding activity; however, there is no getting away from the fact that occasionally it just makes us feel bad. Whilst we may hear spiritually uplifting stories during the course of our research, sometimes we may witness terrible things, things that will anger, scare or distress us. No matter how hard we may try, it is difficult to predict the range of emotions that we may and will experience during our work. However, what should now be clear is that every research project involves emotional work: at one and the same time, we have to deal with others' emotional reactions and confront our own feelings, be they negative or positive. Thus, as many of the vignettes in this chapter (and those that follow) demonstrate, social science research involves a balancing act. As researchers, we have to balance our desires and emotions with those of our research participants, which requires more than a little empathy, a not inconsiderable amount of intuition and skill, and may involve some very hard choices.

Notes

1 Arguably, there are some good reasons for this, not least being that researchers want their reputations to be established on the basis of their academic outputs (ideally papers published in prestige journals) rather than on any emotional difficulties (or indeed pleasures) they may have encountered along the way.

2 Cystic fibrosis is a genetic condition which affects both the lungs and digestive system and results in death in young adulthood.

3 Most patients with CF have to perform rigorous daily treatment, which is often intrusive and time-consuming. This typically includes medication, dietary supplements, nebulized medication, and regular chest physiotherapy. Patients often neglect physiotherapy, which has profound effects on the progression of the illness as it increases the chances of developing chest infections, and can cause irreparable lung damage.

4 HD is a degenerative neuropsychiatric disorder that involves loss of control of voluntary movements, personality changes, cognitive impairment and depression. Because of its typical mid-life onset, it is often described as a 'genetic time bomb' which 'remains dormant until the

person reaches adulthood'. All offspring of an affected individual have a 50 per cent chance of inheriting the genetic mutation that causes the disease. There is no prevention or cure, and death typically occurs about 15 years after onset.

5   Woodward, *Guardian*, 20 May 2002.
6   Harvie, D. (2000) Alienation, class and enclosure in UK universities, *Capital and Class*, 71 (Summer): 103–32.

3
Self

As is the case with all forms of social interaction, research interactions are influenced by who we are, what we are, where we are, and how we appear to others. Yet, as Coffey (1999) has observed, despite (qualitative) research entailing personal, emotional and *identity* work, all too often research methods texts have remained relatively silent when it comes to talking about the ways in which our presence actually affects the research process (see also Sword 1999). Following Coffey's lead, this chapter explores the influence of self and identity on research, focusing upon two main issues: the effect of our presentation of self at various points during our research and the degree of control that we actually have over the ways in which our research participants perceive us.

Managing self or cultivating identity

At the most fundamental level, all social science research is based upon the existence of a degree of trust and reciprocity between ourselves and our participants. The contributors to this first section discuss the role played by self-presentation in the development of trust, empathy and reciprocity within our research relationships. Like Oakley (1981) and Finch (1984), these contributors also highlight some of the ethical concerns that may accompany this process.

The chapter opens with a piece by Abby Lippman in which she suggests that the ways in which we decide to present ourselves to our study participants (for example, by opting to wear one type of clothing rather than another) may influence the types of information and insights we subsequently gain. Whilst Lippman suggests that 'matching' ourselves with our participants may help to develop trust, rapport and the subsequent disclosure of information, she also questions whether we sometimes go too far in our efforts to highlight commonalities in our experiences and backgrounds. As Lippman observes, however important it may be to cultivate the right sort of image and impression when we engage with our participants, it is also important that we feel comfortable with who and what we are.

Appearances can be deceptive

Abby Lippman

It may seem trivial, even frivolous, to consider clothing when one is embarking on something as serious as data collection; the content of one's research report, not one's closet, should lead to (or away from) promotion and tenure. But could it be that what one wears is actually relevant to what one learns? That thinking about clothes and interviewing together provides some lessons about research principles? That appearances are (necessarily) part of the research process?

My thoughts about the connections between things sartorial and qualitative research begin with an anecdote: my parents' announcement of their first visit to me in Canada. This visit was to occur about three months after I'd first arrived here when it would be, on their calendar at least, almost winter – winter with an underlined capital W. For almost everyone who has not lived here, visions of Canadian winter seem necessarily to include mountains of snow, dark days and frigid temperatures. And my mother, having these visions, had packed woollen clothes, lined mittens and heavy-duty boots for her October visit. These visions also led her to pose non-stop questions throughout her visit about how I was keeping warm and whether I had enough sweaters, socks, hats and such to protect me from her worst expectations of what the coming months would be like.

I managed these early queries easily, but then came the real challenge: her offer (which sounded like a mandate to me) to take me shopping so she and my father could buy me a fur coat, something they knew I did not have – and would never buy for myself. What does one say to solicitous parents who only want to protect their daughter's health, their view of what a fur coat keeping me warm would do.

No matter that the mere thought of ever wearing fur gave me serious chills. And no matter that I was, at the time, an adult with two children of my own. A simple 'no thanks' wouldn't suffice; turning down their offer would, I knew, be heard as a graceless dismissal of their concern for my well-being. Frantically trying to find a way to be gracious, yet firm – convincing and compelling at the same time – I grasped onto the straw of the PhD research I was about to begin. 'Mom, I will be going to interview women in their homes, and many of these women are likely to be quite poor. How could I possibly arrive and talk to them wearing such an expensive luxury? Won't my plain woollen coat be more appropriate?'

Fortunately, my mother's social conscience was stronger than her conviction that I could be warm and stay healthy only if wrapped in fur, and we were able to spend the remaining hours of her visit sightseeing and otherwise enjoying the city rather than shopping.

I have had little occasion to think about this episode during the past 25 years. However, some recent experiences working on a project to understand more about women living with a diagnosis of breast cancer brought it to mind. And with hindsight, it seems to offer a chance to reflect not only on clothes per se, but on how appearances in general may be relevant to interviewing.

For example, have any others who may regularly wear jeans (or designer-label suits) purposely reached for something else when setting out for an interview? Trivial and superficial matters, perhaps. But given that we must go clothed to the interviewing situation (participant observation at nudist camps excluded), is there something to be learnt from our 'what to wear' choices? Do these choices really matter?

Certainly, appearances contain class, gender and other social messages. Each decision (do I wear fur or cloth; show my regular jewellery or leave it at home?), if it is at all conscious, represents a kind of second-guessing about the image/impression one thinks one is conveying and the situation we think we will be managing. Do I dress very casually, thereby trying to suggest that I am 'just like' the woman I will be meeting in her home in a low-income neighbourhood? Or do I dress more formally, thinking this will be a sign of my respect for her? Similarly, would more 'business-like' apparel suggest that this is not a regular conversation between two people but, rather, an interview that, no matter how open-ended, I will necessarily be (tightly) controlling?

Do my concerns reflect an implicit assumption that I (as a researcher) have power over the situation we'll be in, while the person being interviewed is merely a 'victim' under my control? And if so, isn't this exactly the opposite of what the feminist principles I want to follow are based on? If I acknowledge that people, in particular the women I interview, have agency, why am I worrying about my clothes and jewellery?

I've been fortunate as a researcher. My empirical work has involved interviewing only women and we've talked about things that are important to them: pregnancy, prenatal testing, genetic counselling, giving birth. Likely, then, what I wore was less important than that I was seen as an adult woman. In these situations, there seemed to be some automatic (and too infrequently questioned) assumption that I'd probably confronted (some of) these same experiences and we could 'share': we were 'alike'.

But what about research in an area where 'sharing' could not be taken for granted? What about appearances in these situations? This leads me to reflect upon a recent project with women living with a diagnosis of breast cancer. In this participatory research project, my co-investigators were women who had themselves experienced breast cancer. These community-based women had had no previous research experience, and our project specifically included a six-month period during which they would get the training they needed to carry out the interviews *they* would be doing. Apart from the political statement we wanted to make about who could 'do' research, my co-investigators felt that participants would talk more easily and openly with them than they might with me, the academic who'd *not* had breast cancer. And since an objective of our research was to explore the nature and extent of women's talk about breast cancer with each other, our method seemed particularly pertinent. In this project, then, the issue was more about 'wearing' a diagnosis, than about wearing clothes.

Without doubt, there are some shared understandings that can only come from having lived similar experiences. I think not only that this kind of 'knowing' is valid and valuable, but that participatory research that builds on it is critical. But, no matter the category of the experience (giving birth; having prenatal testing; getting a diagnosis of breast cancer; and so on), each person lives this uniquely. Thus, no matter how well we try to 'match' interviewer and interviewee, we can still be 'off'. And, I wonder, might we sometimes pay too much attention to the matching and not enough to developing in ourselves, as 'sanctioned' (by our academic degrees) researchers, the listening and empathetic qualities needed to hear women. Could 'disease-matching', like clothes-matching, lead us astray? Are we, in 'matching', trying to play to (assumptions about) an audience instead of just being our authentic selves, in effect worrying more about surfaces than about the depths of women's lives?

It may be more my imagination than reality, but Canadian winters seem to have become much less severe since I first moved here in the 1970s. But if the temperatures and the snowfalls are less challenging, the complexities of research have definitely become more so. There is no simple guide for doing in-depth interviews, just as there is no simple guide for what to wear when doing them. But keeping in mind how easy it is to see through our most opaque clothes, beneath our most clever strategies to 'pass' for something, we might just ask one question when we look into a mirror before heading off for an interview: are we dressed for comfort or to camouflage? My sense is that our best interviews happen when we are comfortable as who, and what, we are, and then listen attentively and respectfully.

Nina Hallowell raises similar issues to Lippman when she recounts an occasion when a woman she was interviewing (about cancer) asked her if she could smoke. Hallowell, a seasoned nicotine addict, describes how she promptly outed herself as a fellow smoker and joined in. Whilst not underestimating the powerful physical and mental effects of nicotine, she suggests that the act of disclosing their (shared) identities as smokers may well have helped in bringing herself (a middle-class academic) and her research participant (a working-class woman with little formal education) closer together, thereby increasing the success of the interview. Like Lippman, Hallowell endorses an open-minded attitude, and she concludes that whilst being comfortable with ourselves is important, making sure that our research participants are comfortable too is imperative.

Smoker

Nina Hallowell

In 1994, I was working on a project that looked at lay perceptions of the new genetics. This involved lots of travelling around England interviewing women in their homes about their perceptions of their cancer family history and their risks of developing breast/ovarian cancer. This project was the first I had undertaken which involved in-depth interviews, and I had quickly learned that, above all else, interviewing requires one to go with the flow. It is the interviewee who sets the agenda – they say where the interview happens, when it happens, and what happens. On a practical level that means: drinking cups of tea when offered, playing with children, tolerating dogs, cats and other assorted furry/feathered creatures who may climb on you or try to eat your tape recorder. You have to take on board whatever is thrown at you and be prepared to consume large amounts of food and drink.

During the first few months of the project, I had drunk my way through countless cups of tea, eaten kilos of biscuits (luckily I have a sweet tooth), sandwiches (mainly ham) and toasted crumpets. My one rule was 'eat whatever is offered, but never ask for anything'. However, up until the day I describe here, I had never smoked during an interview. Indeed, I had gone to great lengths to hide my (guilty) secret.

Concealment of my vice required more than a little forward planning. Normally when doing interviews I would arrive at my destination a little earlier than expected, top up my nicotine levels around the corner, eat a mint and hope that my interviewee would not be put off by the smell on my clothes. Clearly, my concealment strategies had worked thus far, as up until this point most of my interviewees had proudly announced that, as non-smokers, they would not get cancer, an activity, or lack of activity, that I invariably applauded and supported. These statements were not framed in that superior tone that many non-smokers reserve for use with us smokers, but merely stated as a matter of fact. It would appear that no one believed that I, as a 'cancer' researcher, might have succumbed to the carcinogenic weed. However, on a fateful day in November, I was unmasked.

Picture this scene. It was a grey, cold November day. I arrived by train in this little town in Essex. The slight drizzle in the air did nothing to lift my spirits and, due to the vagaries of British Rail, I was running late. I hopped off the train and scanned the horizon for what I hoped would be a bank of taxis. Only one solitary taxi stood in the rank. Weighing up my chances of another cab arriving within 5 minutes, I decided a bird in hand . . . as they say, and jumped in, forgoing the opportunity to get a quick fix. Twenty minutes later, we arrived at my destination – a soulless grey housing estate. By now, I was half an hour late, embarrassed, hassled by the inefficiency of our public transport services, and gasping for a fag. But clearly there was no time for a furtive puff. I knocked on the front door and was greeted by my interviewee. She led me upstairs to her flat, which was warm, bright and inviting but, on quick inspection, very definitely ashtray free.

The tea was made and we sat down to begin the interview. For those of you who have never smoked, imagine the scene. I had now gone for two and a half hours without a cigarette. I was beginning to feel a bit tetchy and caffeine is really no substitute. Biscuits, on the other hand, are quite good in these situations, but there is a limit to how many you can eat during an interview, particularly as the crunching noises often obliterate the quieter bits of conversation on the tapes. So there I was looking at two to three more hours of nicotine freeness, talking about an extremely emotional subject and feeling my concentration ebbing by the second as I fixated upon my withdrawal symptoms.

At the beginning of these interviews, I asked women to talk about their experiences of cancer in their family and their feelings about their cancer risks. This approach normally generated a long narrative that frequently began with a very graphic account of the suffering and death of their mother or sister and finished up with a description of their worries about their own risks. Whilst this method produces rich data, it requires considerable concentration. However, on this particular day, my concentration was severely compromised. The interviewee started to talk about the death of her sister from ovarian cancer following a delayed diagnosis.

Talking about death is difficult for all of us, but when death is unexpected, involves a great deal of suffering, as ovarian cancer deaths frequently do, and comes without much warning to someone you are very close to, it is particularly traumatic. However, despite the emotional nature of the subject, up until this point in the project, all of the women I had talked to had warmed to the theme, and talked at great length, and very movingly, about their experiences and feelings. This woman was different. She was clearly very uncomfortable talking about her sister's death. She spoke haltingly and started to cry. I stopped the tape and then it happened. She stood up, dried her eyes, blew her nose and said 'I am sorry, but this is very hard, would you mind if I smoked?' 'Not at all' said I, thinking there is something not quite right here, it is her house, I have arrived late and proceeded to ask her upsetting questions, and she is asking *my* permission to smoke.

She moved over to the sideboard behind me, opened the cupboard and pulled out an ashtray (complete with butts), her cigarettes and lighter. 'I know I shouldn't do this', she said 'not with all the cancers in the family, but I just can't help myself'. I quickly reassured her that smoking was absolutely fine by me and then, reaching for my own cigarettes, came out as a fellow smoker. A look of amazement came over her face. She said, in a disbelieving tone, '*You* smoke!

But you work in a hospital, and you do cancer research'. Clearly, the very subject matter of my research had marked me out, as I had suspected, as a member of the health police. She sat down, we lit our cigarettes and inhaled deeply, a sense of calm invaded the room. We chatted for a few minutes about smoking, about stigmatization – how everyone hates smokers – and social cohesion – how the best people you meet, generally outside, are smokers. We bonded over our addiction. More tea was made and we resumed the interview. She was still upset, but obviously more relaxed and talked at great length – the floodgates had opened. I too relaxed, it was going well, I was able to concentrate better and be supportive at appropriate moments. I left three hours later after meeting her Mum and drinking two more cups of tea and smoking lots of cigarettes. It was the best interview I had done to date.

Whilst the change in the atmosphere that occurred following our smoking break may have been due to the calming effects of nicotine, I like to think that something else was going on here. I come from a middle-class background, she was working class. I was older, better paid and better educated. To all intents and purposes, we appeared to have little in common, excepting that she had wanted to talk about her experiences and I wanted to listen. As far as my interviewee was concerned, I was a doctor (although I never refer to myself as such when doing fieldwork), and, whilst I am not a medic, I was clearly perceived as an emissary from the clinic that she had attended. Although my smoking habit may not have changed her overall view of me, revealing that I had vices did make me appear more human. Furthermore, our short interlude on the pros and cons of smoking indicated that, at least in a very small way, we shared some common experiences. I believe that it was on the basis of that commonality that she finally opened up and shared her experiences with me.

Life as a smoker may indeed be nasty, brutish and, so we are informed, short, just like that of a contract researcher. However, whilst smoking may damage your health, it is not clear to me that it damages data collection. And before you ask, no, I don't go to every interview with a cigarette hanging out of my mouth. However, ever since that day, when I visit interviewees' homes I immediately check out the premises for smoking accoutrements. If I spot them, I try to work it into the conversation, out myself as a smoker, and give my interviewees the opportunity to smoke. Incidentally, I now have a lot of data on smoking and stigmatization.

Whilst it may well be acceptable to adapt our wardrobes (like Lippman) or indulge in bad habits (like Hallowell) in order to develop a climate of trust, how far should we push the boundaries? This question is raised by Hannah Bradby in the course of documenting her successes and failures in negotiating access to members of a South Asian community on the west coast of Scotland. Bradby suggests that, at times, her identity as a single woman, living apart from her family, obstructed her efforts to gain entry to the South Asian community because it marked her out as 'different', as an 'outsider'. She speculates that her access could have been facilitated had she adopted extreme measures such as presenting herself as married or in the process of converting to Islam (or, indeed, by actually getting married and/or converting). However, as Bradby describes, for both ethical and personal reasons, she was not prepared to go to such lengths.

Finding space in a tight-knit community – qualitative research with Glasgow Punjabis

Hannah Bradby

Some years ago, I conducted a small-scale study of the health of young Punjabi women in Glasgow using participant observation and in-depth interviews. As non-Scottish, non-Asian, and newly arrived in Glasgow, I had no contacts with this minority group. As a single woman without visible family, establishing contacts and credibility with Muslims and Sikhs often proved to be a challenging experience.

'Oh yes, they sent one of these *gori* (fair or white) girls to ask questions when I had my first baby' Mrs Uddin chuckled to her daughter whilst I was conducting an interview with her. My reception from the Glasgow Punjabi community, like Mrs Uddin's remark, was often welcoming, friendly, but mildly sceptical as to the utility or sense of my activities. The warmth with which Punjabi women welcomed me into their homes, places of worship and social lives was combined with various well-intended strategies to rectify my somewhat isolated social status as a student, recently arrived from England and lacking family or friends in Scotland. Over the course of my fieldwork, I resisted some of these attempts, welcomed others and found that my integration into the Punjabi community could only be sustained when its members could accommodate my single status.

On arrival in Glasgow, I started various South Asian language courses, including one-to-one Punjabi lessons with Jasvinder,[1] who had worked as a bilingual interviewer on a sociological survey. I wanted to learn Punjabi so as to be able to include non-English-speaking women in my study. I visited Jasvinder's home weekly, where my lessons competed with other demands on her time, including full-time employment, bringing up her own and her brother-in-law's children, working for the Sikh temple and supporting her self-employed husband. After some weeks, language teaching gave way to informal discussions (or gossip) about Jasvinder's ongoing family crises and problems in the Sikh community. With the exchange of personal confidences, my role as an honorary cousin/sister gradually developed. I was greeted warmly and respectfully by Jasvinder's children, whose homework and revision planning I was delegated to oversee, while Jasvinder taught us all how to prepare proper *roti* (bread) and *chai* (tea). As an honorary older cousin/sister, I was able to take the children on outings to parks, cafés, cinemas and theatres. I was also given the opportunity to accompany Jasvinder's family to weekly sessions at the *gurdwara* (Sikh temple). Being seen to have respectable sponsors gave me both credibility within the Punjabi community and invaluable access to the temple community for my research. Nonetheless, one of Jasvinder's husband's aunts, reputed as a match-maker, could not resist periodically offering to set me up with a 'nice village boy' from the Punjab, if only I would grow my hair and wear lipstick!

Other contacts did not develop so successfully. Myriam (recruited to the study via her GP) introduced me to the local mosque women's group. Christened Deborah Rogers, Myriam became a Muslim as a young adult, prior to marrying the son of a migrant from Pakistan who ran her local corner shop. The women in the group initially assumed that I must be following a similar religious path to Myriam and that I perhaps already had a secret Pakistani boyfriend. They looked for indicators of my faith developing in changes to my clothing and conduct, changes that did not take place. Perhaps if I had become a Muslim, my weekly participation in this group would have led to the development of lasting friend-ships and a wider range of contacts within the Punjabi community. However, despite having a university education and sharing a single status in common with many of the women, this did not happen. The male elders had reluctantly agreed to the women's group meeting in the mosque and the women felt a continual need to prove the devout and serious nature of their meetings. My presence as a non-Muslim outsider threatened the group's credibility. Despite our paths crossing at the nearby university, I failed to become friends with any of these young women. Their own need to be seen by other Muslims as honourable and upstanding, despite being unmarried and at university, left no resources for them to accept me into their group.

Forming friendships with Punjabis was often easier to achieve when my own family became 'visible' to them. My mother agreed to chaperone me on a study trip to the Indian subcontinent that included visiting the relatives of my Glasgow friends. This transformed me in the eyes of the community from an apparent orphan, with no discernible social connections, to a daughter and a sister who had obligations towards and received support from her kin. Follow-ing my study trip, conversation would often include enquiries about my family. Given the importance of kin to Glasgow Punjabis, the presence of my own family rendered me into a 'proper person', and thus a legitimate member of the community.

The extent to which it is possible to gain access to a group as an 'outsider' is unpredictable and not entirely in the hands of the researcher, although a researcher can take steps to maximize her chances, for instance by learning the appropriate language, dressing and behaving in the correct way, and 'hanging out' in the right places. However, some things that affect access cannot (or at least should not) be manipulated for the purposes of a research project – for instance, marital status and religious affiliation. When a researcher fails to get access, the reasons behind this should be considered and respected in terms of the group's characteristics and values as well as those of the researcher.

The problems and challenges that are raised by being (or being seen to be) an 'outsider' are also discussed by Khim Horton. She describes how an earlier encounter with racism (when Horton was mistaken for someone from Japan) influenced her self-presentation in a recent UK-based research project in which she recruited older people from a day centre. When she first introduced herself to potential participants, Horton found herself volunteering that she came from Singapore (a British colony during the Second World War). On reflection, she realized that she had made her ethnic origins explicit because she wanted to be regarded as an 'acceptable outsider' so that she might increase recruitment to her study.

Being a 'foreigner': obstacles to doing qualitative research

Khim Horton

Despite my vast experience as a qualified nurse and a nurse lecturer, I still worry about the ways other people perceive me. This concern originally stemmed from an incident that occurred when I was a student nurse some twenty years ago. An elderly male patient asked me if I was 'a Japanese'. I was quite taken aback at the time because no one had asked me that question before. I suppose where I came from – Singapore – this was not an issue because people could tell who was Chinese and who was not. After I regained my composure, I asked him why he had asked about my nationality. He told me that we (meaning Orientals) all looked 'the same', and that he'd had friends who had fought in the Far East. He'd heard about the horrific atrocities incurred by the Japanese. Realizing that he perceived me in a negative way – as someone from Japan – I was quick to tell him that I came from Singapore (a British settlement which was later captured by the Japanese). His attitude towards me changed immediately. He smiled, patted my arm and apologized. I could sense the warmth and friendliness in his eyes. I smiled back at him, relieved.

The following account illustrates how this previous encounter influenced the way I presented myself in a qualitative research project conducted for my PhD. In this, I explored the ways in which the meaning and experiences of falls are constructed by older people who have had falls and by their key family carers. I decided to target a population of older people living in the community, and included only those who lived alone. From my nursing experience, I knew that day centres and sheltered housing would provide a useful source for my sample. I arranged to spend a week in five different day centres in order to get to know the attendees and to recruit (eligible) people to my study.

My initial meeting at the first day centre did not go as smoothly as I had hoped. I introduced myself to Sally, the manager, when I arrived. After a brief chat, she offered to show me round and, as we went through the door that led to the day room, I noticed that some attendees had arrived, and were sitting, waiting for their hot drink and biscuits. Since I was only going to be at this day centre for a week, I was determined to make the best use of the time available to recruit people to my study. Five older men were sitting at a table in the far corner of the room talking to one another. Sally was about to introduce me to them when the phone rang. She excused herself, leaving me on my own with these men.

John, a bespectacled man, introduced himself and asked me if I minded him asking what I was doing there. I assured him that I didn't mind his question and proceeded to tell him and the others the purpose of my visit, which was to find out if any of them had experienced a fall. John immediately told me that he had not. I looked around and noticed that a couple of the other men were quietly sussing me out. They weren't welcoming, nor did they ignore me. They just 'looked' and said nothing. From my past training, I knew I should be comfortable with 'silences' since they allow people 'thinking time'. But, something about the way these men looked at me made me feel nervous and uncomfortable, like an 'outsider'. There I was, much younger than they were, and 'foreign'. Without really thinking, I found myself volunteering that I came from Singapore years ago to undertake my nurse training, and that 'I'm not a Japanese'. The warm overtures that followed assured me that my remark had gone down well. A couple of the men volunteered that they'd never been to Singapore but had heard it was a very nice place. Some wanted to know if I was still in nursing and if I had been home to Singapore. I didn't feel like an 'outsider' any more.

I have frequently asked myself why I felt the need to tell these men that I came from Singapore. In truth, I think I wanted to be welcomed and accepted by them – for personal reasons and to improve my chances of recruiting them to my study. The way I interacted with these men was almost certainly influenced by the incident that took place when I was a student nurse, far away from home and in a strange country. That incident made me realize (and worry) that my looks (and my accent) could be a disadvantage – particularly if they meant that I was confused for someone from Japan.

More recently, I have started to wonder if my assumptions about other people's reactions to me are always well founded. Over the years, my grasp of English has improved (though it is still not perfect). Should I still be worrying that my accent is a barrier to my interactions with others? Perhaps I have to learn to recognize that when older people ask me to repeat things (as sometimes happened during my research) this may simply be because they are hard of hearing, as opposed to them having a 'problem' with my accent. At the back of my mind, I am aware that I may have developed such an 'inferiority complex' that I could be reading things into situations when they are not there. I think if I do similar research in the future, I will tell my older participants about my perceived problem with cultural differences and accent. Maybe they would value seeing the 'human' side of the researcher.

Susan Eley, like Khim Horton, describes how she unwittingly became the target of overt, and covert, racism when she, an English person, moved to work in another country – Scotland. With great humour, she recalls a number of incidents when she was made to feel not only very 'different', but also unwelcome by (some of) her Scottish research participants. She also details some of the strategies she has developed over the years to either hide her English identity or to cultivate a more acceptable or appealing identity. Whilst she describes how the real, or imagined, cultural differences between herself and her research participants sometimes hampered her research efforts, she also observes that on occasion being seen as an 'outsider' may have been an asset.

Surviving as a Sassenach in the field

Susan Eley

First contact

A young woman sat in an office based in a hospital in the East End of Glasgow. She shared this office with three other contract researchers. She was making telephone calls, 'cold-calling', about participation in a health survey. The work was repetitive and many people hung up. For example:

SE: Hello, I'm telephoning from the University about a forthcoming survey of Glaswegians about their health . . .
P1: Where are you calling from?
SE: The University.
P1: But you're English.
SE: I have called you as part of a random sample of people living in Glasgow . . .
P1: No, I'm not interested.

The young woman, myself, had lived in Scotland for two years. The ways that *some* Scots, men and women, positioned themselves as being different from the English was experienced on a daily basis. This included the handing over of English bank notes 'to take back home' and questions such as 'Why are you here?', 'How long have you been here?' and 'Do you like living here?' With less subtlety, my landlady's 3½-year-old son once said to me: 'You're a dirty Sassenach and I'm a Scotty dog.'

I will now present some of my experiences during a time of 'settling' into Scotland and into qualitative interviewing as a researcher in Glasgow in the mid-1990s.

Doing the first interview

Moving on from earlier experiences, I decided to send out letters to people who had responded to the research features and advertisements as a delaying tactic to exposing my 'Englishness'. On receipt of replies, I further delayed a verbal one-to-one by sending out a letter with possible dates for interview and asking the participants to reply again in a pre-paid envelope with the most suitable date for them. This stalling made me quite uncomfortable as I knew the day would come when I would have to approach the interviewees directly. The day did finally arrive for going out into the Scottish field. Nervous, I picked a 'nice' address in the West End of Glasgow for my first interview in this study.

I worried about what to wear. I decided on black jeans, black boots, grey shirt and smart black jacket. I 'prepped up' on how to 'conduct' the interview, the skills encouraged by standard textbooks. The need to appear relaxed and be a good listener who does not interrupt. Someone who ensures that similar topics are covered in interviews, allocates an equal amount of time to each topic and remains flexible. Someone who is able to 'monitor' their own actions, behaviours and comments.

I arrived at the address, parked my car and rang the doorbell. An older woman opened the door and asked to see my ID card. This being satisfactory, the naïve researcher was invited into her home. There was certainly plenty of 'visual and auditory distractions' discouraged by the textbooks. I felt awkward as I entered the sitting room at the top of the stairs. Memorable were the collection of engraved silver quaich[2] on a walnut sideboard, oil landscapes of Munros[3] on the walls, a Black Watch tartan carpet and a Royal Stewart tartan three-seater sofa and matching chairs.

The older woman was relaxed and asked for further information about the study, about the interview and whether she would be contacted again. We chatted for some time, and with the 'ice broken', I unzipped my bag to retrieve the paraphernalia of interviewing. She hurried out of the sitting room through the other door and came back in with plain grey woollen rugs. She then proceeded to lay them down on the floor, asked me to sit up and then placed them over the sofa, saying that she wished me to be 'comfortable' and not 'scared of the tartan'. I felt privileged that she should 'care' about me, but ill at ease nonetheless.

The interview focused broadly on food and drink. I had just started the section about food preferences, when she jumped to her feet and said 'now would be a good time for a bite' and disappeared into the galley kitchen in this mews house. She returned with a three-tier cake stand with tablet,[4] shortbread and some meringue nests with raspberries and offered them to me. Considering which was the 'lightest' (there was a year's fieldwork ahead!), I plumbed for the fruit nests.

P2: I just knew that was for you, they are very popular with 'visitors', I mean not visitors to me but rather visitors to my country, how long have you lived here?

SE: Two years.

P2: And you haven't developed a taste for shortbread yet – shame on you!

Not wishing to offend I picked up a piece and ate it first – worries about my food intolerance seemed less important than completing my first interview successfully.

Settling in troubles

By the end of 1994, I had conducted around 40 interviews in Glasgow and had become accustomed to the 'you're not from around here?' as a stock question from interviewees. One particular interview, conducted in late November, had a significant impact on me. I had contacted the participant several times by letter giving information about the study, the consent form, the payment and the interview place, date and time. In the study participants were given the choice of being interviewed on the University campus, at the hospital-based offices or in their own homes. This woman, who had experienced job loss, wished to be interviewed at home. I arrived at the pre-arranged time and parked my car across the road. I had learnt not to park outside people's homes after several people had commented that people would think a social worker was visiting. The woman, in her 30s, opened her door and I greeted her. She appeared surprised and anxious. Aggressively she said: 'But you're English. Don't come in. I have never had a Sassenach in my home before and I'm not starting now. You'll have to come round the back.'

She pointed to her side gate. I proceeded through the gate to a small concrete area. I felt deflated. This was winter and I was not well dressed for the outdoors. She brought out a kitchen chair for herself and unlocked an outside store for a plastic chair for me. I asked her if she was concerned about issues of confidentiality as we were speaking outside. She said that she was fine. The interview lasted for only half an hour. It lacked the usual 'prompting' and 'probing' from the interviewer, who elicited short, brusque replies from the interviewee. I felt 'frozen out' physically and emotionally. I was glad to move on.

Surviving in the Scottish field

By autumn 1995, I had interviewed over one hundred Glaswegians. By then, I had an arrangement with a network of cabbies to ferry me to and from interviews at a phone call. This proved easier in terms of not presenting myself in a car with English number plates, having the worry of its safety and drawing attention to my Englishness before I'd even started.

One day in December 1995, I set off to a scheme in north Glasgow by taxi. As we arrived at the block of flats, the cabbie warned me to look out for dogs.

I entered the flats and climbed the stairs, which had a liberal coating of dog mess, and rang the door bell of the participant's flat. A woman in her late 20s answered the door and invited me in.

P4: You're not from Glasgow then?

SE: No East Coast. . . .

P4: Aye I could tell from your accent, thank god you're not from round here, come in and let me tell you what has happened to me since. . . .

This proved to be one of the most successful interviews I carried out for that study. The interviewee was able to discuss intimate aspects of her life because I was a stranger and an outsider who had a limited status in her life and her community. It was 'safe' to talk to me about sensitive issues such as debt and its collection, managing families on a budget and 'keeping yourself going' while living in poverty. Our relationship existed purely for the sake of the research.

I did share some of my experiences with her and with the other women *and men* in my first study in Glasgow. This was not to seek intimacy and friendship or in some belief that I could change the power relations in the research relationship. I shared parts of my life with interviewees as a way of creating and controlling the interview situation. I wanted to make sure that we would concentrate more on the issues surrounding income and food and less on tensions (for some people) about the English in Scotland.

> 'From a Scottish perspective an English national identity is one which is very often understood as being quintessentially "middle class" and is often contrasted with, and provides reinforcement for, Scots' sense of themselves as being much more "proletarian" in nature and outlook'.[5]

Reading my fieldwork diary commentary on the interviews, I realize that within a year I had designed a survivor kit bag of staged stories to prevent myself getting into (imaginary) trouble. These slithers of my life and heritage were drawn from my 'stock of knowledge' about some Scots' interactions with English people.

When I was interviewing P4 in the north of Glasgow, I found myself not being myself but 'doing myself'. I played a more proletarian role by playing up that I was the grand-daughter of a Geordie miner and union steward. I told how I did not live in a flat or house in my early years but in a caravan travelling around a variety of rural areas. But I could, and did, play an alternative myself. In the affluent areas of Glasgow, interviewing men and women of similar class and status as P2, I found myself playing a 'middle-class' role. I was the farmer's daughter from a Tory shire in the east of England, grammar school and university educated, working at a hospital for a university department on a comfortable salary, talking about the importance of property, investment and entrepreneurship.

But, more importantly, from my previous experiences of doing interviews, I had learnt that I did not have to combat an anti-English stance in every single research encounter. Reviewing my field notes, it only occurred in about one quarter of the interviews. Where antagonism did occur, usually dressed up as curiosity or humour, this could be partially dissolved by drawing upon my Scottish capital. My Aberdonian great-grandparents, my childhoods in Orkney and Dundee, and being a Scottish graduate have all helped to some extent. As I rehearsed my stories with one of the cabbies, he added, 'All the English have a Scottish granny somewhere in their past – well the ones that are alright do.'

Having settled in Scotland for a decade now, I am resigned to the fact that some Scots will delight in giving me English banknotes in my change and ask me how long am I staying for. I am English to a certain degree. I accept that I am 'different' from some interviewees' expectations. The encounters highlighted here were difficult experiences, but I haven't let these exceptions taint my enjoyment of going out into the Scottish field.

All the contributors so far have reflected, to a greater or lesser extent, on how we present/manage/cultivate aspects of self so as to develop an atmosphere of acceptability and trust between ourselves and our research participants. Susan Robinson, in the concluding vignette in this section, explicitly raises this issue when she shares one of the strategies she has developed when she undertakes home interviews. She describes how she deliberately tries to cultivate a trustworthy persona by leaving her belongings unattended in full view of research participants when she goes to use their bathroom. As she suggests, if we demonstrate that we trust our participants with our possessions (handbags, recording equipment and so on), they may in turn trust us with their words and experiences.

Handbags and lavatories

Susan Robinson

Trust is a popular concept in contemporary social sciences, and is arguably one of the most important factors in the formation of a mutually productive and socially acceptable researcher-respondent relationship. When I began to go out into the field I appreciated that the interview situation can be scary for respondents because it may involve them making themselves vulnerable through talking about mentally and emotionally charged issues.

However, I found that I had not been considering all potential forms of respondents' vulnerability or the many aspects of trust. Specifically, I had never considered that respondents might see *me* as a tangible threat to them or their property. While the literature frequently refers to ways that the researcher should protect herself when in the field, it rarely deals with whether the respondent is equally protected. I had never considered this until one middle-aged woman I was interviewing in her home said that her daughter had been concerned that I was coming – I might be a thief, or even a murderer.

Later in the day, I thought about this brief comment and reflected on how respondents might see me and what I could do to dispel their fears about my integrity. While all respondents were obviously welcome to have someone with them during my visit, to check my credentials or to turn me away at the door, I realized that there was little I could do to reassure them that I was not going to physically harm them. But I did think that I could do something to ease their minds regarding the likelihood of me pilfering during the interview.

First, I put myself in their shoes. In common with many other researchers, I always accept the offer of a cup of tea; it seems polite and drinking it during the interview makes the interaction seem more like a conversation and less like an interrogation. Picture scenario one: The respondent goes into the kitchen to make the drinks, leaving me alone in another room where I am at liberty to look at, and possibly steal, their belongings.

Next, scenario two: Invariably, drinking a cup of tea means that I will need to use the lavatory when the interview is finished, especially if I have a long drive home. This usually means that I am directed upstairs unaccompanied where, in theory, I have the opportunity (if I am quick) to go into bedrooms and take things. I realized that, in order to expand the trust relationship, a degree of reciprocity was required.

I decided that, all things considered, it would be a most subtle, but nevertheless striking, gesture if I left my handbag where it was in the interview room when I went to the lavatory. In this way, I was placing my belongings at risk in a similar way to my respondents. They would have three minutes to go through my bag, just as I would have the same time to rifle through their drawers. At the risk of sounding like an accomplished villain, I want to stress that I have never considered taking away anything that belonged to my respondents apart from their data.

I cannot admit to having evaluated this technique, systematically or otherwise. No one ever remarked that I had left my handbag, and I have no idea if they even noticed. Therefore, I do not know if my attempts at establishing trust and reciprocity contributed to the quality of the research relationship. Perhaps this would be an interesting question for future enquiry. On another level, I realize that this entire tract is largely oriented towards female researchers, based on the assumption that considerably more women than men carry handbags. Nevertheless, if it is suitable, other items such as briefcases can obviously serve the same purpose. Further, as a woman, I do not know first-hand of the problems male researchers face when interviewing people, particularly the elderly, the ill or lone women, in their homes. It may be that men encounter more intractable issues relating to threat, vulnerability and trust than can be dealt with here.

Obviously, no researcher should put her/himself in a position where s/he feels unsafe or threatened, and in many situations it may not be appropriate or wise to leave one's belongings unattended, or even to be alone with a respondent. We all know that there are no hard and fast rules in research, but the one thing we should all keep in mind is that the need to establish trust does not end with the possession of a signed consent form.

The vignettes in this section bring a key question to the fore, namely how far should we go in order to get the data we want? Whilst it is indeed possible to present ourselves in ways that make us appear more acceptable to our research participants, thus maximizing our chances of gaining access to the field and/or collecting good data, we should remember that there is a very fine line between intentional and calculated self-management and outright deception (a dilemma routinely faced by those doing participant observation research; see, for example, Humphreys 1970; Hammersley and Atkinson 1995). We need to be mindful of the fact that the relationships that exist between our research participants and ourselves are frequently characterized by asymmetries in power and expertise (see Chapter 5). Thus, when striving to (appear to) correct this imbalance and/or to further our research agenda by cultivating a particular persona, we need to take care that we do not abuse our relationships with our participants.

Who exactly am I, and what am I doing here?

Whilst the previous section concentrated on cultivating a particular identity or managing self-presentation in an effort to engage research participants, the contributors to this second section recount instances when their identity – how they are perceived by others and/or how they perceive themselves – has created particular problems and challenges during the course of their work.

The section begins with a vignette by Melissa Nash in which she details her experiences of undertaking an ethnographic study of a creative workshop for people with learning difficulties. During her study, Nash experienced a role conflict frequently encountered by those undertaking participant observation research (see, for example, Spradley 1980; Hammersley and Atkinson 1995; Lawton 2001). Nash, by virtue of her choice of methods, was required to be, at one and the same time, an active participant in group activities and an impartial observer of these same activities. In attempting to reconcile this conflict, Nash concludes that it is important to gain some balance between one's role as a researcher and one's responsibility as an empathic human being. This, as Nash's account suggests, may mean juggling our research interests with our responsibility to the people we involve in our research.

Getting the balance right: doing participant observation research with people who have learning disabilities

Melissa C. Nash

My PhD involved a study of people with learning disabilities who were partici-pating in creative workshops run by an arts company, Proteus (a pseudonym). Because I wished to disrupt group activities as little as possible, I made the decision early on to 'tread lightly', relying predominantly on participant observa-tion as my methodology. Consequently, I worked as a volunteer in these work-shops, assisting and performing alongside other members of Proteus, at the same time as collecting observational data for my thesis. Occasionally I looked after people while they were having epileptic fits or if they needed help using the toilet. The aim of the workshops was to produce performances and installa-tions. On average, about eight people with learning disabilities attended each week. The group followed a similar pattern each session. There would be a warm-up, followed by improvisations, games, massage, or movement and dance work. The session would end with a 'cool-down', usually taking the form of relaxation exercises. I joined in all activities.

A popular misconception is that learning-disabled people behave offensively or dangerously most of the time. Whilst this is not the case, it is true that, like those in the general population, some of them 'misbehave' some of the time. Thus, an important issue that arose during my research was whether or not I should intervene in response to their more 'challenging' or 'risky' behaviour, for example aggression, self-injury, destructiveness and non-compliance.

This issue was raised most strongly by my involvement with Gail, a 38-year-old group member whom staff described as extremely 'challenging'. Although Gail was the least involved member of the group, she was one of the most disruptive. She constantly tried to subvert group activities, often through anarchic behaviour such as violence towards others or public nudity. Gail seemed very aware that removing her clothes in front of others provoked strong reactions, and that this would result in the activity/group descending into chaos while staff tried to regain control of the situation. She had a reputation for biting and scratching, and on one occasion was reported to have taken a 'large chunk' out of the arm of a staff member who had tried to prevent her from stripping. It was felt that Gail needed individual support in order to participate in group activities, and staff informally appointed me to the role of 'containing' Gail.

Gail would describe what she was going to do before she did it. For example, she would say that she was going to take her shoes and socks off, then she would do so, almost as if she were challenging me/others to stop her. When she was about to strip naked, she would say 'I am too hot', and flap her clothes up and down, looking at a person in authority with a sideways glance, challenging them to restrain her. I tried to discourage her verbally, but she did not always take any notice. This raised a dilemma for me. As a researcher (and a person opposed to oppressive practices), I did not wish to 'control' her, but I also realized that, if I took a passive 'observer' stance, she would turn to more authoritative members of the group to test the boundaries of her behaviour, which often met with a punitive response, in the form of separation from the group.

I tried to resolve this dilemma by treading the middle ground with Gail, only discouraging her behaviour when her actions would severely disrupt the group (such as when she stripped off all of her clothes). However, this strategy affected her behaviour in unanticipated ways. Over the weeks, Gail became very friendly with me, holding my hand and wanting to be physically close to me during most of the sessions, and her developing relationship with me began to dominate her involvement in the sessions. Thus, I found myself cast into the role of Gail's advocate during the sessions, helping her to engage in activities and form some connection to other group members, a role I found difficult to reconcile with that of observer.

Doing participant observation research is riddled with dilemmas. As an observer/researcher I did not want my presence to affect the group dynamics I was attempting study. But as a participant – a volunteer – I often found it impossible to avoid being drawn into relationships with members of Proteus, thereby changing the context of my research. I tried to do the 'right thing' for my research participants, even if this was at odds with my research. In Gail's case, I did not want to 'control' or 'contain' her (as had happened to her during most of her earlier life living in institutions), I merely wanted to prevent her from being ostracized from the group. In doing what I saw as the right thing, I often found I had to compromise my research role.

The types of role conflicts Nash describes are not confined to participant observation research. Laura Potts also draws attention to the difficulties of separating our role as researchers from other aspects of our lives, such as our political beliefs and values. Such a difficulty came to light when she was an interviewer on a study which looked at the views and understandings of people who had been refused loans from the British government's Social Fund. Most of Potts' research participants lived in extremely impoverished circumstances, were angry, bewildered and confused, and were clearly struggling to comprehend the bureaucracy. As Potts describes, she found herself torn between her supposed role as a 'detached' interviewer and her strongly held convictions as a feminist and political activist. Like Nash, Potts decided to do what she saw as the right thing, which in her case was to offer advice and support to those she interviewed, even though this meant that her 'interventions' potentially influenced the research findings.

In debt in West Yorkshire

Laura Potts

It certainly wasn't the worst job I've ever had: I got out and about; I had a fair degree of autonomy; I was using my brain, and meeting people. But it lodges in my memory as one of the most personally challenging pieces of work, and probably the most overtly compromising. And for a long while it put me off doing any empirical research at all, unless I had complete control of the design and methodology – which was unlikely, given my novice status.

Over a few months, in the summer of 1990, I interviewed people who had applied for a grant or loan from the Social Fund, had been refused, and had asked for a review of the decision which had also concluded that they were not eligible. At the time of the research, the Social Fund had been fairly recently instigated by the Thatcher government (in the UK) as part of the reforms of social security introduced in 1988, and it already had a reputation, amongst claimants and the Left, as an egregious piece of legislation. Payments from the Social Fund for 'exceptional needs' were to be made available through an application process, and were given at the discretionary judgement of officials from the Department of Social Security. Two-thirds of the money paid out by the fund was in the form of 'budgeting loans'; this prefigured the worst excesses of neo-liberal ideology by demanding that the very poorest people in society who applied for financial help to meet basic needs, such as basic furniture, a cooker, a fridge, should receive only loans they must pay back.

The project was set up to investigate the experiences and understanding of people who had been refused these loans, often on the grounds that they were a 'credit risk' – nicely begging a circuitous question about the nature of poverty. The rhetoric informing the policy changes had claimed that the process would reduce dependency, make people more 'responsible', and be 'empowering'; I suppose this is one of the classic instances of the hijacking of the language of the libertarian Left by manipulative sound-biters of the Right.

The credentials of those initiating the research were sound and I still have great respect for them, for their work and their well-earned reputations for social policy research that makes a difference. But it seemed none of them had any idea what it would actually be like to meet these people and to hear their stories – or if they knew, they weren't telling. The research findings, later published in book form, make no mention of the invisible interviewers at all. Naïvely, I suppose I thought they would be out there in the field too, interviewing someone else nearby. I had no idea that they would just be sitting back at base camp, making what sense they might of the data we collected. I travelled all over the most deprived areas of West Yorkshire, equipped with street maps I had to get from local council offices, and a borrowed car. I had managed to get a friend, with similar recent qualifications, onto the project as an interviewer too, and so we would try to arrange the schedules we were given so that we could be in the same area on the same day. Otherwise there would have been no one with whom to share what was heard, no one to know which street you had gone off to when you were hours late back, no one to map read through the unfamiliar maze of bad housing.

The people whose stories I listened to were confused, angry and desperate – without exception. They had been refused 'budgeting loans' from the Social Fund; they had been refused at review. They still had no furniture, or whatever it was they had tried to get, and they had been demeaned by the whole process. We were supposed to find out whether they understood the review process, which was, inevitably, Kafkaesque, byzantine and bewildering, even to those of us exposed to teaching about social policy. But what I found most intolerable about the whole process was that we were not allowed to offer any insights we might have, or might acquire, about the system, for, of course, this might bias the findings. Nor were we supposed to answer direct questions about what we did know: research was a one-way flow of information. Fresh(ish) from my postgraduate research experience, I knew this was nonsense, and that many feminists had challenged such an approach, and so I broke these rules of instruction on any occasion that it seemed appropriate, justifying my mild deviance with thoughts of Ann Oakley interviewing women (inevitably, our 'interviewees' were almost exclusively women), and in the hope that it might enable an interviewee to argue her case more effectively, or help someone else to do so for her.

Asking people why they thought they had been refused the loan inevitably brought responses about the lack of understanding, the hardness and lack of sympathy of the officials, who were seen to inhabit another world, not an account of the system and its guidelines that the questionnaire wanted. In order to distance myself both personally and politically from these unsympathetic officials, I needed to establish some different credentials, to show actively that I cared about the respondents' situations: to show which side I was on. So I would reply to questions they asked me, as best I could, about how the system worked, why some people got money and others didn't. Sometimes, too, I would suggest where they might get help and advice locally, if they didn't already know. I began to have a hunch that there were some times of the year when there seemed to be more money in the system.

These were just minor ways of expressing a profound disquiet with the whole process, and it seemed in accord with other work I was doing at the time: running Women and Health classes in community centres, being a very active member of a Community Health Council and challenging District Health Authorities on behalf of patients who were getting a less than fair deal, and working to get the first self-help breast cancer groups set up against the wishes of the surgeons. But nothing I had read or heard or previously done gave me any guidance on how to act faced with lives and situations that were so intolerable, and perpetuated by iniquitous state policy. As I drove away home I would rant aloud with frustration – aware, too, that of course I had the privilege to leave those estates, to get away.

I still have very vivid pictures in my head of those places, and of the stories I listened to, of women crying and apologizing, of their kids sitting silent and still. Sometimes, when I'm teaching research methods classes, or running a seminar on the ethics of research practice, I describe what I found doing this interviewing, and students are as shocked as I was. I remember the family who had been refused a loan to buy beds for the children, despite the fact that they were sharing the one bed in the house with both parents; the woman who took me into the 'kitchen' and showed me an empty space, a standpipe in the middle of the floor: she had been refused money for a cooker. There was a catalogue of stories of dealing with local loan sharks and the consequent mess of debt and fear. These were the families who were dubbed the 'underclass', too poor even to receive state help as there could be no likelihood that they would ever pay back the money for the bunk beds or the cooker.

I still don't know what I should have done to do this better: being tamely if instrumentally subversive seems like playing the game really, a kind of complicity. The published findings include verbatim quotes from some of the stories, and they do come across as strong expressions of the injustice and humiliation that applicants experienced, and give some legitimate status, then, to their views. But I think there are still important ethical issues to be addressed in this kind of work: should the researcher be merely asking questions about knowledge and understanding, particularly when the topic is acknowledged to be one that has already caused distress to the respondents? Wouldn't it be more appropriate to ensure that interviewers are able to give accurate and useful information if it is requested, that research is not just one way? Doing this work did clarify for me, subsequently, that I wasn't interested in research for the sake of research, as an academic exercise or as a job. And so it has been: I've managed, for the most part, to keep my activist and academic work informing each other. And perhaps, too, reflecting on that summer of interviewing in the process of writing this account, it sharpened my conviction that qualitative research should allow people's voices to be heard, and directed some of my own work to finding ways to do that. I am in debt, still, to those respondents in West Yorkshire.

Rosaline Barbour, reflecting back on a long and varied research career in which she has used both participant observation and interview methods, describes experiencing similar role conflicts to Potts and Nash above. She also describes instances when she has been aware of a degree of misperception about her role, and admits, on occasion, to feeling that she had no choice but to collude with her research participants' misapprehensions.

Reinstating the researcher

Rosaline S. Barbour

Although we are fond of emphasizing the importance of interaction when carrying out qualitative research, it is easy to overlook the importance of the roles that our respondents assign or construct for us in the process. Attempting to view oneself through their eyes may be helpful as a research tool in interpreting our data, but it can make for some uncomfortable 'home truths'. Having been involved in hands-on research for around 25 years, I have recently begun to reflect on this phenomenon; in particular, how my research persona has evolved over time.

As an undergraduate researcher carrying out a participant observation study of a religious sect, my main concern related to the ethics of attending informal gatherings where many participants were likely to be unaware of my research agenda. My research interests were often viewed as irrelevant in the grander scheme of things, a common response to my attempts to 'out' myself as a researcher being: 'It doesn't matter what brought you here, we're all drawn by a variety of things . . .' Being the same age and moving in similar circles to many of the sect's members reinforced this perception of me as a fellow 'seeker of enlightenment'. I encountered similar issues when carrying out a participant observation and interview study of a cohort of students undertaking social work training. Although, in this instance, my 'respondents' had a greater awareness of the research process, there was, nevertheless, an underlying assumption that I was in some way predisposed to viewing the world through a lens sympathetic to the philosophy of social work. Because I conducted my fieldwork in a small city, there were many occasions when my research and private persona overlapped – social networks frequently coincided. In the course of both studies, my research contacts often introduced me to their friends as 'a devotee' or 'someone else doing the course'. Whilst my acquiescence in the face of such mildly fraudulent descriptions left me feeling vaguely uneasy, I could see that it had simply been too tortuous for my informants to furnish a more detailed explanation of our relationship.

Looking back, I realize that I colluded with participants in presenting a naïve, earlier or less well-formed version of myself. Although this strategy has made it easier for me to elicit and listen to their views, at times it has made me feel acutely uncomfortable, and has led to many private doubts and recriminations. Although these problems were particularly marked in the early stages of my career (when I conducted a prolonged stint of participant observation), they have also arisen in subsequent projects. For example, I have frequently found myself listening politely and non-committedly to interviewees while they have expounded views that I (as a private individual) have found disturbing or unacceptable – such as racist or sexist tirades.

Another scenario that has given me cause for concern has been when I have found myself – with a mixture of relief and unease – colluding with interviewees who have treated the interview encounter with some scepticism. In some situations, interviewees have gone along with my schedule, whilst providing a commentary which has assumed that the questions involved have been imposed upon us both, as 'reluctant compliers', by some higher and less clued-up authority. At the same time, I did little to dispel these misperceptions. Such an approach has been helpful in allowing me to pose questions without overly threatening rapport with respondents, but has meant that I have often felt that I was being slightly dishonest. That people have found it so easy to assume that I had been told what to ask them has also, at times, undermined my confidence in myself as a competent researcher.

I had assumed that people's perception of me as a novice researcher would be short-lived. However, perhaps due to a combination of my (hopefully) unassuming interview style and gender (female), this persona has had a long shelf-life. Indeed, it is only fairly recently – probably once I reached my mid-40s – that people's view of me has appeared to change. Even if I am not necessarily seen as an 'expert', I am finally seen as responsible for selecting my own interview questions and research topics.

Having for years worried about the ethics of colluding with a 'novice researcher' ascribed persona, I initially breathed a sigh of relief at this newfound credibility. This feeling, however, has proved to be short-lived, as my new research persona has given rise to a new set of dilemmas. Recently, I have been involved in carrying out interviews with couples undergoing investigations and treatment in relation to sub-fertility. In stark contrast to my earlier work with respondents of my own age, this has involved me as a middle-aged woman talking to much younger people. Perhaps this marked difference has served to highlight more clearly the different ways in which respondents may perceive a researcher. The semi-structured interview schedule was designed to follow couples' progress through the system and elicit their views and feelings. However, I was rather unnerved to discover that some of these couples took the opportunity to engage in 'emotion work', in which they speculated, in what appeared to be an unscripted and exploratory way, on the future of their relationship. This involved them expressing their feelings directly to each other, whilst continually looking to me (the researcher) as a witness to these exchanges. I sensed that some response was required of me, but also felt unnerved, as my research training had not exactly prepared me for what increasingly appeared to be a counselling role. Interestingly, the much younger researcher who carried out the bulk of the projects' interviews did not find herself exposed to similar exchanges. I can only conclude that my age and demeanour had led my respondents to assume that I had some expertise in this sphere. Ironically, the young researcher was the one who had been on the counselling courses!

This messy business of confronting and seeking to understand my own discomfort has persuaded me of the impact that our evolving biographies and changing personae can have on our research. In other words – just when you think you've cracked it, you find yourself groping to make sense of new and unexpected challenges!

The key message of Barbour's vignette is that it is sometimes impossible to second-guess how others will perceive us and that, despite our best efforts, our research persona may on occasion be beyond our control. Marion McAllister has a similar tale to tell. During her research with individuals who were at high risk of developing colon cancer, she had occasion to interview a number of people who seemed unwilling to accept that she was a social science researcher (rather than a medical professional working at the hospital where they were recruited). As McAllister describes, she went to great lengths in her attempts to 'correct' their mistaken assumptions about her identity, and felt considerable unease when her efforts were rebuffed.

On the joys and sorrows of recruiting hospital patients

Marion McAllister

Medical research ethics committees usually require researchers to recruit patients through hospital consultants. In my experience, this can sometimes lead to confusion, in that research participants may identify the researcher with the hospital, regardless of how explicitly the patient information sheet (and the researcher) states otherwise. This happened on a number of occasions during my PhD research, a qualitative study of predictive genetic testing for a hereditary cancer predisposing syndrome.

In this study, the first contact with recruits came through a letter from their consultant in cancer genetics. Because of ethics committee requirements, this letter had been composed by me, but printed on hospital headed notepaper, and signed by the consultant. Enclosed with the letter was an information sheet, also composed by me but printed on hospital headed notepaper, and a consent form accompanied by a pre-paid envelope addressed to myself. The information sheet made it explicit that the research was being conducted for my PhD, and that I was based at the University of Cambridge's Faculty of Social and Political Sciences (that is, a non-medical department). It also stated that the proposed research interview had nothing to do with the patient's medical follow-up, and that participation or non-participation would not affect the care they received from the hospital in any way.

Recruitment proceeded well. Some of the recruits (most typically those who were highly educated) appeared to have a very good understanding of what I was hoping to achieve. These participants seemed very interested in what I was doing, and keen to help in any way they could. They were also very supportive of my attempts to gain a higher degree. Indeed, some spoke proudly of their own children's academic achievements, and were keen to show me their graduation photographs (we were usually sitting in the parlour). I gained the sense that an element of middle-class self-congratulation had crept into their interactions with me, and that their agreement to take part in my research formed part of the way in which they liked to present themselves to the outside world. Small compensation, perhaps, for their family history of cancer. But not all my recruits were the same, and my hardest and most challenging experiences arose when I felt alienated from a participant by a wide socio-economic and educational divide.

One participant in particular created a number of challenges and concerns for me. Barbara (not her real name) came from a large family in which a cancer predisposing mutation was segregating. Barbara's mother had died from cancer at a young age, and Barbara's education had been cut short by the need to nurse her mother through her illness, and later to support the family after her mother's death. From my relatively privileged vantage point, Barbara's life history was tragic. As well as having a number of close relatives whom she had witnessed suffer and die prematurely from cancer, she had fallen pregnant outside marriage at a time when society was a lot less tolerant of single motherhood. She had later married the child's father, who went on to develop serious health problems, and Barbara had spent most of her adult life working very long hours as a cleaner to support her husband and children. I got the impression that her marriage had not been very happy, and that this was just one more thing that Barbara had accepted as her lot in life, along with her increased risk of developing cancer.

What particularly struck me was the gratitude Barbara expressed on each of the three occasions I went to interview her. I am almost certain her gratitude stemmed from the fact that (despite my best efforts) she identified me with the hospital, where she was having a predictive genetic test. Indeed, each time I went to see her, something always happened that made me feel that it was necessary to clarify my research role. For example, she might say to her daughter, 'It's the lady from the hospital'. I would explain (again and again), that I was not from the hospital – I was from a university in a different city. I had come to talk to her because I was interested in how her family had coped with the family history of cancer and how they were now coping with genetic testing, and that I was nothing to do with her hospital care. She would smile at me every time and say: 'Yes dear, you're very good to come and see me . . . everyone at the hospital has been so nice . . . coming to see me . . .' I tried repeatedly to clear up the misunderstanding, but sometimes I felt I was verging on being rude or argumentative if I challenged her yet again about whom she thought I was. It also felt rather pompous to keep insisting I was from Cambridge University and was doing a PhD.

Every time I interviewed Barbara, she treated me with the greatest respect, even subservience – which rather embarrassed me. She overwhelmed me with gratitude for visiting her, and for listening to her talk about her situation and her worries and concerns, about how she and others in the family were coping, and about her life history and her family history. At times, she would stray onto other subjects that worried her: her husband's health, his outbursts of frustration about his mobility problems, and his drinking, as well as her daughter's relationship problems. I would always try to gently steer her back to the question of genetic testing. I got the feeling that Barbara was not used to people listening to her, or giving her permission to talk about herself and what she had been up against in her life.

Each time I left her, Barbara forced a little present on me, thanking me over and over again, and mentioning 'everyone else' at the hospital and how nice they had all been. I was mortified by this, because from my point of view, she had nothing to thank me for. Despite everything I did, I don't think that Barbara ever separated me in her own mind from her hospital care. Not only had the hospital put her in contact with me, she had been visited at home before by a genetic counsellor, as part of her hospital care – someone who had listened to her and who had talked about her family history. Perhaps it felt a bit the same for her when I visited her; maybe she saw our interviews as therapeutic. The concept of research seemed unfamiliar to her, and I even suspect that the difference between a university and a hospital were in some ways lost on her. She had not gone to university and none of her family had done so either.

The Little Oxford Dictionary tells us that to exploit means to 'use or develop for one's own ends; take advantage of'. Did I exploit Barbara? I suppose, in a way, I did, although I tried not to. She gave me very good data – I was the one who ought to be grateful – but it was clear that she thought I was there representing the hospital, to offer her support. I felt that, in some ways, recruiting patients using hospital-headed notepaper was partly responsible for this misunderstanding (although Barbara's confusion also seemed to stem from the fact that she had had home visits from hospital personnel in the past). But then, perhaps, in her own way, and perhaps not deliberately, Barbara had exploited me too. She was certainly very grateful for what she got out of our interactions. Being trained in genetic counselling, I am very aware of how similar a research interview of the kind used in my PhD can be to aspects of genetic counselling. And so, perhaps it should come as no surprise that research participants do find these sorts of research interviews therapeutic. Perhaps we should acknowledge this as something positive that participants can gain from taking part in research. Maybe we should also acknowledge that the people we recruit can often have hidden motives for their participation, motives that might not always be clear even to themselves, rather than pretending to ourselves that they always do it out of pure altruism.

Being a researcher and being yourself

Presentation of self or identity management is a fact of life – we all do it all of the time (Goffman 1959; Crossley 1995). However, in the context of our research, the ways in which we present ourselves to others, or are perceived by others, raise a range of ethical dilemmas. Presenting ourselves as sharing attributes with our research participants may well make the relationship (feel) more equal and reciprocal, but is this always our only motivation? As the result of our efforts at self-presentation, our research participants may feel more comfortable and respected, but they may also give us better data. As researchers, surely we have a duty to avoid deceiving our research participants about what we are doing, why we are doing it and who we are?[6]

So how far should we go to cultivate an acceptable persona, and to what extent are we prepared to compromise our own beliefs and values in the process? As has been noted above, when engaging with our research participants we need to balance both their needs and our own motivations. Research interactions exist purely for the purpose of research and thus, arguably, to present them as anything else is ethically questionable (Dunscombe and Jessop 2002). At the same time, however, as some of the vignettes in this chapter suggest, if we can improve our research participants' lives – for example, by giving them the information they need or by appearing to befriend them for a short time – wouldn't it be wrong not to do so?

Notes

1   All names are pseudonyms.
2   Scottish drinking vessels.
3   A series of Scottish mountain peaks.
4   A Scottish sweet, rather similar to fudge.
5   McIntosh, I., Robertson, D. and Sim D. (in press) 'We hate the English except for you, cos you're our pal': identification of the 'English' in Scotland, *Sociology*.
6   For an example of a highly controversial piece of covert research, see Humphreys (1970), who posed as 'watchqueen' in order to observe homosexual encounters in public toilets.

4
Others

Research is ultimately a collaborative endeavour. Whether we work as part of a large research team or on a project we design and conduct on our own, our research will necessarily entail contact and negotiation with others. As this chapter serves to demonstrate, whenever and wherever this contact occurs, we will need to achieve a balance between our interests, the interests of other people, and the interests of the research itself.

In this chapter, the contributors describe the impact that other parties may have at different points in the research process, and the subtle and complex negotiations which may be required in order to keep everyone happy. The chapter is divided into three sections. In the first, the contributors highlight the ways in which other people may influence the conduct of our research, either by regulating our access to the field or by being less than responsive once we actually get there. The vignettes in the second section focus on the rewards and challenges created by collaborating with others on research projects. Whilst working as part of a research team can create welcome opportunities for intellectual stimulation and emotional support, successful team working, as our contributors suggest, is also dependent upon achieving a balance between the competing needs and interests of all team members. The final group of vignettes is concerned with other people's interests in the outcomes of our research and, more particularly, how we may need to manage these interests so that we can retain some control over the dissemination of our findings.

Getting started

So we've thought up a great idea for a project, got our supervisor's go-ahead and/or secured funding; now all that needs to be done is to go out there and actually do the research. This sounds easier in theory than it is in practice. Indeed, the four vignettes in this section detail some of the problems we may encounter when trying to gain access to the field, either during our negotiations with gatekeepers or when we are trying to gain the acceptance and trust of our research participants.

In the first vignette, Lesley Lockyer documents various obstacles she encountered when trying to get her qualitative research project approved by a Local Research Ethics Committee (LREC).[1] The LREC she dealt with did not appear to understand the basic premises of her research, resulting in a frustrating and drawn-out process of negotiation and renegotiation for all concerned. Luckily, Lockyer survived to tell the tale, and puts her negative experiences to positive effect by suggesting strategies for dealing with ethics committees in the future.

What happens when the LREC does not understand your research design and methodology?

Lesley Lockyer

When I meet other health service researchers we bond when we share experiences of submitting (qualitative) research proposals to LRECs. This vignette relates one of my all-time worst experiences and what can be learned from it.

In October 1995, I began a PhD that looked at women's experiences of living with coronary heart disease. During the planning stages, I met with the Chair of the ethics committee. He commented that he hoped I would be undertaking a substantive piece of work and not 'just a spot of interviewing'. Apart from that, he was generally supportive and indicated that the proposed study would almost certainly be approved.

At that time, the majority of the ethics committee members were consultant physicians and surgeons. There was only one nurse on the committee, but she was also acting as my sponsor. All submissions (unless submitted by medical consultants) were required to have a sponsor who acted, to a lesser or greater extent, as a supervisor. This role was usually taken on by a medical consultant. However, since I aimed to have a nursing focus in my research, I chose the only senior nurse from the Trust who had the background to fulfil the sponsor's role. This meant that she could not participate in the ethics committee's deliberations.

I submitted my application in May 1996 and received a response six weeks later. At this point, I realized a new Chair had been appointed. To my horror, it was a man I knew by reputation, renowned for his research, but also for his strongly held convictions about the nature of 'science' and 'scientific research'. To say that qualitative research was anathema to him would be unfair; rather it simply did not exist.

I still have the letter sent by the committee administrator. Six years on, the comments continue to arouse feelings of horror and humour. They revealed that a number of the committee members were totally ignorant about qualitative research. To be fair, not all of the comments were negative (a couple of committee members even supported the study). The main areas of concern were that the study only included women, had a qualitative methodology and that there was a potential for researcher bias.

So the pressure was on me to respond to the committee's concerns. The first problem they raised was that I specifically wanted to research women. In my original submission, I had highlighted that most previous research on coronary heart disease had been undertaken on men. In my response, I stressed the lack of research on women, I repeated that I did not want to introduce a group of men (for control purposes, as they had suggested) as virtually all previous research had focused on men, and (as I had also stressed in my first application) I would be able to use published results from these studies as a comparison.

The committee's second concern was with the qualitative nature of the study. Three members simply viewed qualitative research as unethical. Comments were made about the hypothesis (there was no hypothesis), the lack of a control group and the poor experimental design. One member commented: 'This submission looks like bad science, and therefore is not to be supported on ethical grounds'. I responded to this by highlighting the fact that qualitative research was methodologically and ethically sound and that prestigious medical journals regularly publish the results of qualitative research.

The last area they raised was around the potential for researcher bias during the interviews. I felt this was an important area for discussion. Two committee members implied that I would suggest to the women I interviewed that there had been a gender bias in their treatment and, in doing so, I would be doing these women a 'disservice'. At this point, the thought crossed my mind that some of the committee members' comments were less to do with ethics and more to do with avoiding litigation. In my original submission, I had been careful not to suggest that I wanted to interview the women only about their hospital treatment, emphasizing throughout that I intended to explore their experience before their diagnosis and referral to the hospital as well as any in-patient stay they may have had. I re-emphasized this and crossed my fingers.

I submitted the revised proposal and, again, I received a negative response. Apparently, the committee still felt that a male control group would strengthen the research. At this point, the Chair proposed that someone other than his medical colleagues should be given the opportunity to review my proposal. The committee administrator seemed quite pleased to inform me that it had been sent to a lay member of the committee who apparently specialized in the area of animal welfare. I felt that perhaps a social scientist would have been of greater use, but I kept this rather dangerous opinion to myself. My concerns were confirmed when I was shown a fax from this particular committee member suggesting that the research proposal would be improved if designed as a randomized trial!

I was getting rather fraught by now. I was into the second year of my doctorate and seemed no nearer to beginning data collection than when I started. Discussions with my supervisor began to centre on how we might find an alternative sample of women with heart disease.

Finally I went and had a long talk with my sponsor and we decided to see the committee Chair together with a third submission. The Chair requested that I make minor alterations to the original proposal. In the final analysis, the only change I had to make was in the first paragraph of the consent form and a sentence in the information sheet. I removed a statement that suggested equal numbers of men and women suffered from coronary heart disease. The Chair read the amended proposal and approved the study. This interview lasted all of ten minutes.

So what can be learnt from all of this? With the benefit of hindsight, I should have set the pace more than I did. I should have made an appointment to see medical colleagues who I knew were sympathetic to my project to ask for their advice. I should also have used my sponsor more proactively. By letting the ethics committee set the agenda, I played into the notion (expressed by the administrator) that what I was doing was not as important as the medical research they usually consider.

I recommend getting to know the Trust's Research and Development Department and the ethics committee administrator as soon as possible. In fact, get to know them well and learn who is on the committee and how it works. If you need a sponsor on the committee, find a lion not a mouse and use them. Being self-effacing may be a wonderful quality in general, but it is not going to help you if you want to get your proposal through an ethics committee.

Steven Platt also encountered various difficulties negotiating ethical approval for a (postal) questionnaire study. In Platt's case, ethical approval was contingent upon a change to the study's recruitment procedure, one that seemed to put people off volunteering to participate, thereby plunging the whole project into jeopardy. After Platt realized that things were going wrong, he had no choice but to go back to the ethics committee. Like Lockyer, he has some important lessons and insights to share.

Impediments to survey recruitment

Steven Platt

I am a principal investigator on a research study funded by the Medical Research Council (MRC), which was designed to assess the implications of organizational change for the health and well-being of National Health Service (NHS) staff. The study uses a quasi-experimental design, taking advantage of a 'natural experiment' of organizational restructuring and change in the NHS secondary care sector. Outcome evaluation is being undertaken in part through repeat surveys of a cohort of staff in six NHS teaching hospitals (Trusts). Putting this aspect of the research design into practice has not been straightforward.

What we wanted to do

In our grant submission to the MRC, we proposed that data should be collected by means of a self-report questionnaire that would be distributed to the sample via the internal mail of each participating Trust. Potential participants would receive a letter advising them about a forthcoming invitation to participate in the study. The letter would be distributed by the Trust, ensuring that the research team had no access to any names or other information about the sample. About a week later the sample would be sent a package consisting of the question-naire, an information sheet, consent form and self-reply envelope. Following at least one reminder to the whole sample, non-return of the questionnaire would be interpreted as refusal to participate. No change to this procedure was demanded by the MRC following peer review.

What the ethics committee asked us to do

Following the MRC's indication of willingness to fund the proposal, we submit-ted an application to the ethics committee. This closely followed the design and procedures described in our MRC application. Much to our disappointment, it was sent back for revision. The ethics committee raised several concerns. Foremost was an objection in principle to the proposed recruitment procedure and an insistence on a more explicit 'opt-in' procedure.

How we responded to the ethics committee's objections

Under revised arrangements, we had to use a two-stage procedure. Trusts were to issue invitations to participate *via* a pack that contained a letter of invitation, an information sheet, a consent form and a reply-paid envelope. A staff member wishing to participate was expected to return a signed consent form to the research team. The consent form asked for the person's name and home address, so we could now send them the questionnaire.

The information sheet made it clear that, while confidentiality was an abso-lute principle, anonymity was limited in the sense that the research team would know details about respondents (for the purposes of follow-up, arising out of the study's longitudinal design). However, it was emphasized that no data on individuals would be released and Trust management would not know who was/was not participating in the study.

How successful was this recruitment process?

Despite significant efforts to maximize response rates (holding planning meetings with senior managers and staff side representatives prior to the start of the baseline survey, advertising the study in Trust newsletters and on posters displayed in key sites across the Trusts, holding meetings and setting up display stands, and so on), under 10 per cent of the target sample were recruited into the study. The vast majority of those who returned their consent forms subsequently completed and returned their questionnaires. The main problem was the failure to persuade most of the sample to return the consent forms.

Back to the ethics committee

Our response rate was inadequate, both relatively and absolutely. We had insufficient data to undertake a statistically meaningful analysis. Consequently, we had no choice but to go back to the ethics committee.

How did we account for the poor recruitment rate?

We speculated about the reasons for our recruitment problems and came up with the following:

- The recruitment procedure required by the ethics committee expected too much of respondents in terms of time and effort (they were required to fill in and separately return two sets of forms).
- Some invitation packs may have failed to reach their intended destination.
- Some staff may have failed to notice the invitation pack.
- Some staff may have been insufficiently motivated to take part.
- The marketing of the study may have been inadequate, so that some staff were effectively being approached 'cold'.
- Concern about identification (non-anonymity) of individual respondents may have been a deterrent to participation.
- The information sheet may have put off some would-be respondents, due to its length and detail.

Negotiating with the ethics committee

During the pilot stage we had achieved a significantly higher response rate using a one-stage recruitment approach. We therefore assumed that the *main* cause of our recruitment problems was the cumbersome two-stage approach originally requested by the ethics committee. Thus, we entered into negotiations with them to go back to some variant of the original design. We proposed that, on a new census day, a sample of staff would receive a study pack, consisting of an invitation to participate, information sheet, consent form, reply-paid envelope *and questionnaire*. Respondents who wished to participate would be expected to return both consent form and questionnaire. (We would have to exclude from the achieved sample those who failed to return the consent form.) No reminder would be sent. Refusal would be registered passively, by not responding to the invitation.

In considering our request, we urged the committee to bear in mind the main features of this study:

- Use of an observational design (that is, no intervention or invasive treatment of any kind).
- Respondents would be staff members, not patients.
- No information about staff would be made available to us by the Trust (we would only receive such information from respondents themselves, which is required for the purposes of follow-up).
- Respondents were guaranteed unconditional confidentiality.
- Respondents would not be coerced into participating in the study (receipt of the questionnaire together with the invitation to participate does not invalidate the intention to seek informed consent; in fact, it can be argued that consent will be *more* informed in as much as staff would be able to assess directly the acceptability of the questionnaire).

Much to our relief, the committee accepted our arguments and authorized the revised 'one-stop' approach.

The new recruitment phase: more of the same

New samples were drawn up by the Trusts and invitation packs were issued. Although a final estimate of the response rate has still to be calculated, it is apparent that recruitment of the second cohort has been more successful – but only marginally so. We have failed to meet the ambitious target of recruiting over 50 per cent of staff to the baseline of the cohort study. We were so convinced by the circumstantial evidence of resistance to a two-stage recruitment process that we placed most of the blame for our problems on the ethics committee that had originally insisted on this approach. We tended to dismiss other possible barriers to participation. Now, as a result of the difficulties with recruitment of the second cohort, we are altogether less sure about where to point the finger of blame.

One probable cause of our difficulties is research fatigue, resulting from the proliferation of surveys launched at NHS staff prior to and during the period when we were in the field. On the basis of evidence from a process evaluation (also conducted for the study) and discussions with colleagues involved in NHS-based research, we would also suggest that we seriously underestimated the negative effect on participation caused by the need to request personal information from respondents. In order to be able to examine changes in perceptions of the NHS environment, and in health and well-being, over time at an individual level we had no choice but to gather such information. But did we do all that we could to allay understandable fears that partial anonymity might compromise unconditional promises of confidentiality? In the current climate within the NHS, we probably did not. In targeting key partners and gatekeepers (Trust managements, staff sides, the ethics committee) with whom successful collaboration was essential, we tended to overlook the importance of working more closely with would-be respondents to understand potential barriers to participation from their point of view. The evidence of ever-falling response rates in health surveys, whether conducted in communities or in organizations, suggests that this is a lesson that may be more generally applicable.

As Platt's and Lockyer's vignettes serve to highlight, when things on our projects appear to be going wrong, we should not be afraid to approach the people who may be (intentionally or unintentionally) obstructing our research. Despite our best efforts to explain our research to others, misunderstandings can crop up. Likewise, problems can sometimes emerge during the course of a research project that no one (researchers or gatekeepers) could have anticipated. In such instances, as Platt and Lockyer demonstrate, it is good to talk. Moreover, we should always try to keep in mind that gatekeepers (such as ethics committees) are not simply there to be obstructive and make our lives a misery. Indeed, in both Platt's and Lockyer's cases, perseverance and reasoned debate ultimately saved the day, as both were able to negotiate the type of arrangements they believed were necessary to undertake their research successfully.

The idea that we should not give up too easily when things seem to be going wrong is echoed by Jonathon Tritter, whose research was nearly blocked by the headteacher of a school where he wished to deliver a questionnaire to pupils. In order to reassure this headteacher that his questionnaire was not culturally insensitive, Tritter drew upon his academic credentials and his (extensive) research expertise, thereby establishing himself as *the* expert. Whilst such a strategy might not be appropriate in every situation, Tritter's suggestion that we should try to stand our own ground is pertinent since, as Lockyer has already demonstrated, being too self-effacing can also lead to problems when we need to be taken seriously.

Negotiating access and establishing expertise

Jonathon Tritter

My PhD research explored socialization and the relationship between moral attitudes and religious beliefs and attitudes in school children. I was interested in how children's moral attitudes changed and were shaped by the school they attended. The research took place in three English secondary schools: one Roman Catholic, one Jewish and a 'typical' state comprehensive.

I conducted observational research in these schools as well as delivering a questionnaire to the pupils. I recall many methodological challenges associated with this research, but one in particular relates to the access negotiations, specifically those around the administration of the questionnaire. The questionnaire included a range of scales as well as a lengthy demographic section incorporating a question on religious identity, taken from the Office of Population Censuses and Surveys' Social Attitudes Survey.

I piloted my research at a Jewish independent school and the headteacher kindly gave me an introduction to a well-known Jewish comprehensive. My first letter to this school received a reply dictated to a secretary saying that they received so many research requests that they only accepted those that would have direct benefit to their pupils. My response explaining how my research would be of benefit received no reply at all. Feeling very downhearted, I asked the headteacher of the Jewish independent school to put me in contact with another school. This time I received a positive response. Shortly thereafter, I also successfully negotiated access to a Roman Catholic school through an academic Catholic philosopher who had given me an introduction to the head of the Archdiocese board of education.

So now I had two religious schools in my sample, albeit at different ends of the country. To obtain my third school, I spoke to the Chief Inspector of Schools asking him to suggest a 'typical' comprehensive. He introduced me to a headteacher who seemed willing for her comprehensive school to be involved and who quickly delegated the deputy head to help me.

Whilst I had been successful in getting three schools on board for the observational component of my study, I still needed their approval for administering my questionnaire. Negotiations for administering the questionnaire typically started with the headteacher in each school (I sent the headteacher a copy of the questionnaire and then set up a brief meeting to discuss any issues arising from it). The questionnaire was approved by the headteachers in the two religious schools without any glitches, and I also gained the agreement of the heads of religious studies for me to give out the questionnaire in religious education classes. Having successfully negotiated access for carrying out the survey in these two religious schools, I had no inkling that I was to face a major challenge in the state school. In my meeting with the headteacher of the state school, she announced that she had given the questionnaire to the head of lower school and that I should see her as she might have some comments. I walked over to the lower school and met the teacher in question; she told me that she had shown the questionnaire to a few colleagues and that they thought it was 'entirely inappropriate'. It emerged that the questionnaire had been circulated for comments to: the head of lower school, the head of upper school, the head of religious education, the deputy headteacher with pastoral responsibilities as well as the head of each of the years in the school! Each teacher had carefully added their views (in a different coloured ink), indicating how they thought I should correct the questionnaire to make it more appropriate for the children in their school.

I was flabbergasted. I composed myself and asked the head of the lower school what she thought the main problem was. She flipped through the pages of the questionnaire until she came to the offending question:

> *Please circle the religious group you identify with most closely.*
> *Church of England   Roman Catholic   Methodist   Protestant*
> *Jewish   Muslim   Hindu   Sikh*
> *Buddhist   Other (fill in) _____   None*

She explained that this was a very divisive question and that in her school they taught children that religious difference did not matter. Looking over her shoulder, I saw the helpful suggestion that had been written in by one of the many commentators:

> *Please circle the religious group you identify with most closely.*
> *Christian   Jewish   Muslim   Other (fill in) _____*

My thoughts were of despair, despair heightened by the fact that one of the aims of my research was to investigate the relationship between different types of Christianity. Here, in the 'secular' school, I was on the verge of being prevented from obtaining key information about the relationship between school and religious identity.

I tried my best to appear calm. I replied that I was surprised at the reaction because religious identity was surely an important part of child development and that this question was a key part of my research. The head of the lower school repeated that the question was inappropriate and 'wouldn't the new version be okay?' Emulating my supervisor's tone and deportment, I replied that I had been trained in the oldest sociology department in the United States, this was the third survey I had designed, and I had spent more than eight years learning how to design questionnaires. 'I know what I'm doing', I said, and 'the question really needs to stay in its original form'. 'Fine, if that is the way it has to be' she said. My PhD was saved and my data was collected (but that is another story).

So, I learned that when negotiating access it is as important to establish your own expertise and define the areas that are open to discussion. Daring not to be too humble or too flexible may be the only way to ensure that you access the information upon which your research depends.

As we have now seen, Tritter's success in negotiating access to schools was also strongly reliant upon the goodwill of other people – in his case, headteachers who were willing to put him into contact with colleagues at other schools. Martin Richards also found that he was very dependent upon other people when he was trying to undertake observational research in a special care baby unit (SCBU). As Richards' experience demonstrates, gatekeepers can operate at many different levels within an organization, so just getting approval from the person at the top (in Richards' case the paediatrician in charge of the SCBU) may not suffice to get the type of access we need.

Loitering with intent in a special care baby unit

Martin Richards

I have long believed that an important principle in social research is to have a good knowledge of the context for your research. Taking an example from my recent work, suppose you are designing a study of how genetic counselling may influence a particular group of families, you need to know how a genetic counselling clinic works: who are the key actors, how do they see their roles, what is daily life like in the clinic, how do people come to seek clinic appointments? Some of that knowledge can be acquired by reading textbooks of genetic counselling, accounts by social scientists or patients'/clients' descriptions. But there is another kind of knowledge, one that can only be gained by good old-fashioned ethnography, hanging around, watching, listening and talking to people as they play their parts in the process.

Some years ago I had been carrying out a study of developing mother-child relationships. It was a longitudinal study that recruited mothers during pregnancy and followed them for the first year of their children's lives. This included being present at the birth, which in most cases took place at home. The sample was selected in such a way as to exclude those likely to have complicated births and children who were likely to have major problems. Later, by way of comparison, I wanted to work with a sample of parents with children who were born too small, or too soon, and had spent their first weeks or months in a special care baby unit (now usually called a neonatal unit). The SCBU – or 'scaboo' as they were usually called – was new territory for me. I asked a paediatrician I knew who was responsible for a SCBU if I could visit and he readily agreed.

On my first visit I arrived in time to join the weekly teaching round. A large group including consultants, registrars, junior doctors and a couple of clinical students and senior nurses clustered around each incubator in turn. A junior doctor outlined the clinical history and situation. Sometimes there would be some examination of the baby, but usually simply a discussion of diagnostic, prognostic and treatment issues. I had done a lot of reading about the more common clinical problems, but I struggled with the endless jargon and abbreviations. Looking at the generally very small and immature babies I tried to see if, from their appearance and movements, I could distinguish those who were doing well and soon to be discharged from those who were very seriously ill and unlikely to survive. I couldn't. Almost all of them looked terrible – a very different species compared with the large and chubby babies I had seen delivered at home and watched growing up. Later, after the ward round had departed, some mothers padded in from the ward next door wearing their dressing gowns and slippers. Their presence seemed to normalize the situation a little, though most of them simply sat by their baby's incubator and watched.

In my early visits I decided I would talk to the mothers and the occasional father or grandparent I met in the SCBU. I was told stories of pregnancies and births, and their hopes and fears for their babies. I learned about the pain, anxieties and frustrations of being on a 'lying in' ward with a baby on the SCBU whose care you could not be involved in and could merely watch. With more or less daily visits I got to know a lot about some of the parents and became more attuned to signs of progress – or otherwise – in their babies. I had talked much less with the doctors and nurses and other professionals who came to the SCBU. We greeted each other and I learned their names from their name badges. I asked questions about procedures and equipment I did not understand. I tried to extend these brief conversations, but this seldom worked. People were busy and I sensed some resistance. Perhaps my role was misunderstood. I had been introduced as a psychologist interested in mother-infant relationships. I was clearly not a doctor, or at least not a proper one, so why should I be told things about staff roles or the clinical condition of the babies? It seemed it was fine for me to hang around as a visitor and talk to other visitors, the mothers and other relatives of the babies, but I felt I was being excluded from the business end of the SCBU. Maybe this would change with time, but perhaps I needed to be more assertive in asking staff what I wanted to know? Should I talk about it to the consultant who had invited me in? I began to feel quite down about it all. I just didn't know how to proceed.

One day I received a call from the consultant. A colleague from overseas was visiting who was interested in 'the psychological side of things', would I like to join them both for supper that evening? I would. After the meal the consultant said he wanted to stop by the SCBU to check on a baby and I went back to the hospital with him. I'm not sure quite why, but when the consultant had finished and offered to drive me back home, I said I would stay on in the unit.

That night I learned something very important about scaboos and, indeed, other front-line medical situations – day and night are quite different. There are fewer people around, and the atmosphere is much more relaxed. Unless there are major emergencies people have more time to sit and talk. Professional boundaries become much weaker. There are no visitors. A lot of coffee gets drunk.[2] Home life and all sorts of issues beyond the scaboo are discussed. I quickly found that some of the conversations that had not happened during my daytime visits were easy to have at night. And so I became a night worker. Sometimes there were emergencies and occasionally babies died. When these things had happened during the day, screens were drawn and I felt I should keep out of the way. At night the nurses and doctors seemed to feel I should share all they had to do. Later on I began to stay over the shift changes and resumed my daytime visits. Luckily, what seemed to have become a changed role persisted into the daylight hours. Finally, I had become a participant in the life of the SCBU, not just an observer.

For Richards, it was not just a chance event that led to his situation improving, it was also his willingness to adapt to his research environment (in his case by changing the hours he worked in the SCBU). Thus, above all else, his experience demonstrates how important it is to be flexible when we are reliant upon the time and goodwill of others. Yet, as the vignettes in this section have also highlighted, this type of flexibility may require us to tread a very fine line between accommodating other people's preferences and needs and standing our own ground. We may well need to be prepared to rethink our ideas and/or alter our methods if our original plans fail to facilitate access or generate the types of data we require. However, we also need to be mindful of the fact that if we are too flexible or accommodating in our approach, we may end up doing a very different project from that which we originally intended. Arguably, however, what is most important is that we respect the wishes or requirements of others – gatekeepers or research participants – for without their cooperation and goodwill, access may be denied and our research may never take place.

Getting together and staying together

Doing research frequently entails working as part of a research team or with a range of clinical or other collaborators. Research collaborations, like other types of social relationships, are complex relationships influenced by social, cultural and personal norms. Just as similarities in gender and ethnicity may not be enough to ensure that good rapport is achieved in research interviews (DeVault 1999), a common research goal may not suffice to hold a research team together, never mind ensure that all members work well together. As the vignettes in this section illustrate, working with others is an experience that can be intensely fulfilling and/or deeply challenging, for like all relationships, those constructed for the purpose of research involve both give and take.

The idea that we need to give and not just take when we collaborate with others is central to Liz Lobb's vignette. In order to undertake research with women at high risk of breast and ovarian cancer, Lobb was dependent upon a number of extremely busy (and geographically dispersed) clinicians to recruit her participants. Getting and keeping these clinicians on board required a great deal of time and effort and, as Lobb demonstrates, more than a little imagination. In her vignette, Lobb shares the many ingenious strategies she devised for cultivating and nurturing relationships with her clinical collaborators. She also reminds us how important it is to keep our research collaborators regularly informed about our progress, since, without this kind of (positive) feedback, it would be unreasonable for us to expect them to remain committed to helping us out.

An affair to remember

Liz Lobb

I had just returned from four weeks trekking in Nepal. Little did I know that the planning, team work, stamina and good humour that took me to Everest Base Camp would stand me in good stead for the multi-centre study I was about to undertake. This study looked at the process of genetic counselling with women from high-risk breast and ovarian cancer families. It was a randomized controlled trial of the provision of an audio-tape of the consultation. The project was also to form part of my PhD, so there was an added incentive to invest the time and energy to make it work well.

The study involved collaboration with staff in ten familial cancer clinics around Australia, and therein lay some of the complexities. The distances between clinics ranged from 25 to 1600 kilometres and crossed three time zones.

The courtship

In the early planning stages, I organized teleconferences with all the investigators. These were booked in advance, and allowed sufficient time for an agenda and relevant papers to be mailed, often by express post. I confirmed addresses, telephone and fax numbers and the best times in the day or week for contact. E-mail was invaluable as it was fast and more likely to elicit a response (even on weekends). By the end of the study, we were up close and personal enough to exchange mobile phone numbers.

On Judgement Day I will plead guilty to the destruction of acres of trees. Yes, the dreaded ethics application. I was to learn my first lesson. Investigators are too busy to prepare ethics applications. I had to prepare 12 of them. I obtained some of the signatures of co-investigators by fax, but each hospital ethics committee required an original signature from the investigator on site. I prepared the applications, photocopied them – in some cases 15 copies were required (remember to warn your departmental secretary to order in extra paper) – and mailed them to the investigator who would sign them and deliver them to the research office in their institution.

My next lesson was that while I thought my research question was the most brilliant, innovative and original, and therefore required top priority, it was usually one of several going on in the same clinic. The challenge was to make my study stand out and to make the recruitment process as painless as possible.

Dating

Ethics approval for the study to proceed in all ten centres took nine months. I used this time to prepare a recruitment folder for each clinic. To maximize my recruitment and highlight differences between the studies, I prepared a flow chart of the steps required. I listed eligibility criteria and laminated the sheet so it could be placed on the desk beside the phone as a reminder to clinic staff when a woman rang to make an appointment to invite her on to the study. Labels were made for patient files so staff could see immediately that the next patient was on the 'audio-tape study'. Staff could then make sure the audio-tape machines were on the desk and a blank and coded tape in each machine ready to go.

My *pièce de résistance* was to purchase high-quality tape recorders, small enough for two of them to fit on a desk without being intrusive, yet of sufficient quality (and within budget restraints) to be able to capture every utterance. In my search for such technology I even rang the local police to find out what they used. After all, I'd seen them in all the TV cop shows where the accused is told to answer out loud for the tape. As many people are techno-phobic, I made sure there was plenty of time for my collaborators to practise taping. I listened to the first tape from each clinic and provided detailed written feedback – it was too loud, too soft, too much background noise, too much static, don't place it near the air-conditioner, or in a consulting room next to the hospital's public address system. No matter how careful I was, nothing could have predicted the noise of a cleaner vacuuming that totally drowned out one consultation.

Keeping the flame alive

A deliberate strategy, and the key to successful collaboration, was to keep the investigators informed at all times. I sent them copies of ethics committees' approval letters and of requested changes to the patient information sheets and consent forms. I placed copies of the baseline and follow-up questionnaires that we mailed to the participants in the recruitment folder. This way clinic staff knew what questions we were asking and there would be no surprises if a participant challenged their consultant on the content.

I knew I would be pushing the relationship if involvement in my study incurred any additional costs (aside from time) for the various clinics. I included reply-paid envelopes for the return of audio-tapes and any questionnaires that women may bring to their clinic appointment. Not only did this strategy save staffs' time in writing out envelopes, it also meant I got my data returned as soon as was practical and ensured that no one was lost to the study because of missing data.

I believe the most important strategy that was used to encourage collaboration was face-to-face contact. I sought out opportunities such as conferences or monthly meetings to travel personally to the centres and brief all the staff. At one such conference I invited investigators on the study to a breakfast meeting. It was the middle of winter and Melbourne was bitterly cold. I contacted the functions organizer at the university where the conference was being held and booked a small, well-heated room for breakfast. I organized catering to provide orange juice, plunger coffee, warm croissants, pastries and a platter of fruit. It worked a treat. It was a low-cost conference and breakfast was not included. All the investigators for each centre were present. They all knew one another, so it was a relaxed opportunity for them to catch up. I had not met them all, so we were able to ask each other questions and sort out the logistics of recruitment. We joked about the audio-tape machines that would sit on their desks for 12 months and record their every word. We were able to calculate realistic recruitment figures and identify differences in clinic protocols that needed to be considered. The breakfast concluded with a good sense of camaraderie and enthusiasm for the task ahead.

The study would not have been possible without the cooperation of every member of the team from the clinic secretary to the genetic counsellor, clinical geneticist and consulting oncologist. I undertook what I called the 'Travelling Research Show'. Equipped with overheads, recruitment folders and audio-tape machines I visited each centre. Some days I would travel 1600 kilometres just to have one hour in between patients. I had to be organized, precise but flexible in my briefings.

Once the study began and recruitment progressed, I kept my co-investigators up to date. We required 40 participants from each centre so when 20 were recruited I would send a fax with a cartoon of a bottle of champagne and a message saying 'Congratulations – 20 women recruited – 20 to go!!' As we crawled towards our final recruitment numbers 18 months later, I faxed off short messages (always accompanied by a cartoon) such as 'Nearly there' or 'only one more to go!' I telephoned the centres regularly to see if there were any problems, such as running out of labels or fax forms. I prepared a bi-monthly newsletter to update the team and reported the individual centres' recruitment numbers to get a bit of friendly competition going.

Another strategy in collaborative studies is to negotiate authorship of papers at the outset. I found that investigators needed more than a pertinent clinical question answered or a relevant hypothesis addressed. They needed papers for their CVs. Whenever I felt I was asking too much of their time, I would remember that they needed me as much as I needed them.

Throughout the two-year study I responded to every request to present preliminary data at annual meetings and conferences. All participants in the study were acknowledged on the opening slide, in discussing the study I always used the collaborative pronoun 'we'. I accepted praise and criticism on behalf of the 'team'. I deferred to investigators who may have been present in the audience at question time. However, I embraced the golden rule – the buck stops here – if something went wrong on the study, I always took responsibility.

The ending

When the study was finished I mailed thank you cards and sent flowers to each clinic. I met local clinic staff for lunch and delivered bottles of champagne. When inter-state collaborators met at future scientific meetings we made sure we had a coffee or a drink to 'de-brief'.

We are now collaborating on another study. This one is more geographically central, but after such a positive previous collaboration it was not difficult to get the clinics involved again. The recruitment system works like a well-oiled machine. We take it in turns to organize meetings with the working party, and try to out-do one another with the catering. We meet over lunch, and it is fortunate that one of the investigators has a taste for French wine, another bakes wonderful savoury biscuits, and yet another brings fresh dates, cheese and olives – the hospital cafeteria will never compete.

Research is a meticulous affair, a mutual respect and liking for one another is important, and a common purpose – the 'study' – is essential. But I have found that it is the little things that can pull it all together.

Whilst it would have been impossible for Lobb to undertake her research without a number of collaborators, sometimes researchers work with one another for other reasons. Julie Kent describes the feelings of isolation that researchers commonly experience when working alone (particularly when writing a doctoral dissertation or a book). One solution, she suggests, is to establish partnerships with other researchers. She recounts her experiences of team working, in particular her long-standing collaboration with a fellow researcher with whom she has developed a very productive relationship over a number of years. As her vignette demonstrates, forming long-term research partnerships can be an important source of both intellectual and emotional support.

Team working – have a brandy!

Julie Kent

After I completed my PhD, the pressures to produce publications and demonstrate that I was research active seemed initially to place emphasis on individual achievement. The rather solitary activity of producing a book based on my earlier work reinforced this sense of isolation. Then I met Alex. We discovered that we shared interests around the use of human implant technologies. Since then, we have developed a research programme that explores questions about the regulation and governance of implants as a type of medical device, innovation and the development of new implant technologies and the emergence of tissue engineering. As our research partnership has strengthened, I have found a new confidence in developing research and seeking out new opportunities for projects and publications. One particular opportunity arose in response to an advert to tender for a government-funded project to look at the national breast implant registry data. I decided to phone around to try to locate a collaborator with clinical expertise who might be interested in working up a research proposal with Alex and I.

Cold calling to introduce myself and my research has become much easier to do than in the early years. After a few phone calls, I located an eminent plastic surgeon who had published some papers on breast implantation. He agreed to meet up to explore possibilities for collaboration. He invited me to stay at his home, which though a generous offer, I was reluctant to accept since we had not met and I always find mixing work and social time exhausting. The idea that I would agree to spend the night at a stranger's house to talk about research struck me as rather risky and potentially stressful. So I asked Alex to come with me and we arranged to stay in a bed and breakfast. The plan was that we would have dinner with the surgeon and his registrar. On arrival, we learned that the surgeon had decided to cook dinner for us at his house. His registrar arrived to collect us and take us over there.

Sitting in the thick, padded leather seats of the car that was driven by our newest research contact, we turned into the long drive that led up to the consultant's house. We entered a warm kitchen. A log fire was burning in the centre and there was a delightful smell of dinner. The consultant surgeon, wearing a pinafore apron and bow tie, warmly welcomed us to his home. We admired the house and learned that it had a helicopter pad (and that parking a helicopter in London is expensive!), a swimming pool, games room and much more. Part of me regretted turning down the offer of accommodation.

The occasion was a heady mixture of informality and formality. Though inwardly uncertain about the wisdom of agreeing to this meeting, my courage was strengthened knowing that Alex and I had discussed our agenda for the evening as we travelled up on the train. We had already done a lot of work and the possibility of setting up a collaborative project with clinical contacts was an exciting one. The meal was delicious. While by this time of the evening I am normally too tired to think straight, I tried to keep alert and steer the conversation in the direction of formal business. I had avoided the wine to ensure I maintained a clear head. After introductions, we began to set out our research interests and explain our approach as social scientists. It was clear that, from a clinical perspective, the consultant and his registrar had rather different concerns, but we established that we had an overlapping interest in the policy questions. I was struck by the unexpected feeling that it was rather unusual, indeed, slightly bizarre, to be dining with three men whilst discussing the merits of breast implantation. Although their interests were strictly professional, there seemed something slightly contradictory about discussing breasts in a kitchen by a warm log fire. As a topic of conversation for men, breasts are often linked to sexual stories (or so women assume!) The intimacy of sitting in someone's kitchen could be seen as conducive to intimate talk. Yet, this was a business meeting and breasts in this case were part of the business agenda. As a woman, my perspective on breasts was likely to be a rather different one from the men sat round the table, and had I been on my own I might have felt intimidated by the situation. As it was, having a male research partner was very helpful on this occasion. I felt reassured that I had an ally who could assist in maintaining a degree of formality and act as a mediator. By the time brandy was served, we had agreed to meet the next morning in the theatre suite at the nearby hospital.

Our discussions continued the next day in the 'staff rest room' of the theatre suite, where our clinical collaborator arrived in his theatre greens and white wellies to chat between operations. He invited us in to observe him in action but we declined. Alex looked nervous at the idea (all that flesh and blood!) and I explained that, having worked previously as a nurse, I had been in theatre many times and, in any case, we had a train to catch. It seemed inappropriate to our aims to be drawn into the clinical aspects of his work. Also, we were uncomfortable with the idea of being put in the position of spectator. Would the patients in theatre give their permission for us to be there? As a sociologist I might have found the location of this business meeting rather intimidating too, but since I am familiar with the inside of theatre suites and hospitals I was able to deal with it. By the end of this second meeting, we had agreed to develop a small project that would look at the social and psychological aspects of breast implant surgery and are currently seeking funding for this.

Collaboration with others and team working appear to be essential if you want to secure research funding these days, but these relationships take time and effort to develop. Conferences are important places to make research contacts and to network. After all, it was at a conference that I first met Alex. Alex and I have set up two other international project teams since by advertising on the CORDIS partner search database and as a result of our conference attendance.

As a researcher you need to take some risks, you need to get out there and contact and meet new people (sometimes in the strangest of places). Ultimately, navigating both the formal and informal processes in order to advance a research agenda requires a degree of self-confidence and assertiveness. Whilst the male-dominated nature of the research environment may appear to put women at a disadvantage in this respect, my experiences indicate this is not necessarily the case. For me, talking business over dinner that evening wasn't easy – particularly as I don't drink brandy – but as I have discovered, such occasions are a necessary part of the life of a researcher. However, that evening would have been more difficult for me if Alex had not been present. So my advice would be that 'team working' can open up new opportunities, and research partners can offer invaluable support.

I would like to express my grateful thanks to Alex Faulkner for his support and for giving me such a positive view of the benefits of team working over the years. I hope his experience of working in a team with me is a positive one too and that he continues to enjoy the brandy!

Kent demonstrates that working with other people (such as Alex) can be a very enriching and rewarding experience. However, her vignette does also raise pertinent questions about how far we should be prepared to put ourselves on the line in order to attract and cultivate potential research collaborators. As Kent rightly points out, researchers (particularly female researchers in a male-dominated research environment) need to be prepared to actively seek out opportunities for career development. But, in doing so, as she implicitly suggests, we must take care not to put ourselves into situations where our confidence, credibility and ability to advance our research agendas are threatened.

That working with others can create challenges as well as rewards is boldly (and bravely) illustrated in the vignettes by Clare Williams and her colleagues Priscilla Alderson and Calliope Farsides and by Sarah Cunningham-Burley and Kathryn Backett-Milburn. In the first, Williams, Alderson and Farsides share their experiences of working together on a study that involved a truly interdisciplinary collaboration – their academic backgrounds being sociology, health-care ethics/political philosophy and nursing. Whilst the interdisciplinary nature of this research team enabled the project's complex research questions to be addressed, at times it was also experienced as a source of tension. As all three contributors suggest, they brought their own (disciplinary-influenced) assumptions and research agendas to bear in the research process, and this required considerable accommodation and compromise from all concerned.

Interdisciplinary research: culture clash or the best of all worlds?

Clare Williams, Priscilla Alderson and Calliope (Bobbie) Farsides

Many research programmes encourage applications from interdisciplinary teams. Our research team combined several backgrounds. Priscilla is a sociologist; Bobbie a health-care ethicist and political philosopher; and Clare combines nursing and sociological backgrounds. We found this mix valuable, stimulating and sometimes very challenging.

Our project[3] explored how health-care practitioners addressed questions about genetics and ethics that affected their work. Many of the practitioners worked in areas related to pre- and postnatal care. The study design included individual interviews (undertaken by Clare and Priscilla) and small multidisciplinary ethics discussion groups (facilitated by Bobbie). As the project proceeded, we became aware that we had each approached these discussion groups with different agendas and assumptions about what they would and should be like, which we had never really discussed.

Although our individual perspectives on particular issues, such as women's choices around termination, often resulted in heated debate between team members, it was our differing assumptions about the purposes and running of the discussion groups that generated tensions during the early stages of the project. As the following reflections indicate, the different team members approached the discussion groups with different questions and expectations that were, in part, related to our previous teaching and research experiences.

Priscilla: When interviewing people individually, I sometimes feel uncertain about how far to draw them out, and encourage them to express very clear and sometimes extreme views. This can make the research process and reports more vivid and interesting. I also feel uncertain about how far to challenge people, such as by raising possibly obvious and frequently voiced criticisms of their views, or by pointing out exceptions that qualify their generalizations. On the one hand, I don't want to make interviewees feel defensive or threatened by my responses, since they are helping me, and as research subjects they ought to be treated with respect and be able to feel at ease. On the other hand, if I respond by seeming to accept or even support views that I might disagree with, and if I do not question their views, in a sense I do not give them any right of reply. They might be able to make their case more firmly and convincingly through answering my queries. To encourage people to make extreme and unqualified comments and then publish these in my research reports, with or without adding counter views, could verge into hack journalism, and could make them feel angry or embarrassed about the publication. I try to aim for a middle way of encouraging clearly expressed views and also discussing these with interviewees to elicit their considered reflections. Suppose someone makes a passing comment that hints at eugenics – should sociologists question that, or ignore it?

The problem of whether to accept or to question is less pressing during private individual interviews, especially given the editorial control researchers have over their reports. We can leave out awkward examples. During the semi-public ethics groups, however, I found the question became more urgent, first because of the 'ethics' title, and second because they were groups. Sometimes participants made comments that I thought were eugenic, certainly denigrating about disabled people with inaccurate generalizations. I was very concerned that if we accepted these views without comment, we would appear to support, endorse and even promote them as 'ethical'. At first, I was unsure how we would deal with these situations if they should occur. Luckily, Bobbie was very experienced in running such groups and knew the style and pace that best helped practitioners to start thinking about ethics. I am now convinced that her respectful, non-judgemental and gently probing approach was most appropriate for these introductory meetings, which provided rich research data. The discussion group format made me aware of my need to think more carefully about how to reach a balance between being under- or over-accepting or questioning, and between research interviews being interrogation or discussion sessions.

Bobbie: I had always wanted to get involved in empirical research, and in the past had been frustrated by the abstract and detached nature of much philosophizing. Even applied ethics can seem divorced from reality at times. In all of my work my aim is to talk to people who have the will and hopefully the power to make a difference, not to other philosophers who care only about the elegance of arguments. This project therefore combined two features I value: first, talking to health-care professionals about what they do, and helping them to sort out whether or not this coincides with what they believe they ought to be doing; second, finding out whether the preoccupations of philosophers in any way reflect the concerns of those involved in health-care provision.

Participating in the discussion groups provided me with a unique and invaluable experience. Having taught applied ethics for many years, the group format was familiar to me. I have also had a good deal of experience of working with health-care professionals. However, there were important differences in this case, which meant that I had to reflect carefully on how to best guide the groups through their discussions. Social scientists want to know what people are doing and why they are doing it; philosophers want to discuss what they ought to be doing. On this occasion we needed to combine all these elements.

I felt it was important to remember that our participants had not signed up for a philosophy course, but were assisting us in our research. I therefore felt that the purpose of the seminars was slightly different to those I was used to, and that the terms of engagement might need to be adjusted accordingly. Having said this, it remained important to apply standards of rigour and clarity to our discussions, and do something more than 'find out what people think about . . .' My role was to steer and challenge, but to do so in a way that encouraged honesty and openness, and that was not experienced as threatening or critical. In terms of my experience as a philosophy tutor, I realized that I was compromising slightly when dealing with these discussion groups. I was less ready to expose inconsistencies, less likely to highlight incoherence, and not always willing to push participants into admitting the logical conclusions of their views. Whilst it was sometimes difficult to effect this compromise, I would defend this stance in terms of the fact that most participants were speaking in a more open way than ever before about issues that troubled them, some were grappling for the first time with very complex dilemmas, and others were prepared to voice views they knew to be out of step with their colleagues. Whilst I wanted to encourage this process, I did not want to create further problems for our participants by beginning to explore even more complex issues which could never be resolved in the course of one meeting. In a sense I felt it was enough to begin the discussion and establish a starting point.

Clare: This was my first postdoctoral post, and I came into it with very little knowledge about ethics, genetics, or disability rights. As the group convenor, I felt very responsible both to my colleagues and group participants. I wanted the groups to run smoothly for all concerned. With my own background as a health practitioner, I wondered whether people would find the groups useful or too threatening, and whether busy practitioners would be willing to give up two hours to attend something that might sound a bit nebulous. Although I had faith in Bobbie, a recent attendance at an ethics conference had left me anxious. Some ethicists appeared out of touch with the realities of health care, and seemed more keen to score points in terms of how well they argued, in what seemed a rather detached, abstract way. Although I recognized the importance of this type of debate, I did not think that it would be appreciated by many of the practitioners attending, most of whom had had little, if any, formal ethics input during their professional education or working lives.

I was extremely relieved at the end of the first group, as I felt Bobbie had facilitated it in a way that illustrated her understanding of the complexities of everyday health-care work. She had also focused on some of the key areas that seemed to be most important to the practitioners, as was illustrated by their keenness to continue debating these issues, even after two hours. I was happy with my role as observer during these discussions. However, as the groups went on I became increasingly aware that Priscilla wanted to take a more active part, and that she was becoming frustrated with the pace and content of the discussions.

Working together

At this point we realized that it was time for us to convene a meeting to talk over our feelings about how the groups were proceeding, what we wanted the groups to accomplish and how best we could achieve this. Whilst this meeting required us to acknowledge our different perspectives and expectations and their effect on the project, this brainstorming was useful in that it also reinforced the fact that we shared similar goals and anxieties.

For example, we all knew that inviting practitioners to discuss their moral views and values had the potential to be quite destructive. On the one hand, we wished to challenge them to confront the moral complexities and potential conflicts within their professional lives. On the other, as a team, we felt a responsibility towards them, which raised questions in our minds about the possible destabilizing effect of our work. Acknowledging this dilemma was useful for us as a team. Looking back, we feel that by working together we struck the right balance between our wish to challenge and explore, and our wish to support and help to develop reflective practice in the field.

There were other times during the project when personal differences particularly emerged, new understandings of each others' views were reached and compromises made. At the end of this process we felt much better placed to understand the differences between us, and the ways in which our methods and expectations could sometimes conflict. Although having to explain and defend our own views and methods to one another could be uncomfortable, like the grit in the oyster, it also helped us to clarify our thinking. Overall, we gained an understanding of how combining philosophy and sociology can enrich the gathering, analysis and reporting of the research data, and we are currently working collaboratively on further projects.

Whilst the life of a contract researcher can be 'nasty, brutish and short' (see Grellier, Chapter 5), Sarah Cunningham-Burley and Kathryn Backett-Milburn suggest that project managers do not fare much better. Reflecting upon their experiences of managing projects (separately, together, and with others) over many years, they portray research management as a lonely, isolating and sometimes downright frustrating experience. Whilst Cunningham-Burley and Backett-Milburn adhere to the view that project managers have a duty to try to keep all members of a research team happy, their vignette demonstrates that, no matter how hard we may try, this can sometimes prove impossible.

The ups and downs of team working: reflections on project management

Sarah Cunningham-Burley and Kathryn Backett-Milburn

The days of the lone scholar seem to be long gone for many social scientists, especially those of us who work in multidisciplinary or applied settings and in contexts where income generation is valued almost as highly as research output. Much as we may yearn for the simplicity of having almost complete control of the research process, from project inception, through fieldwork to writing up, we may also forget the isolation and loneliness that can accompany the life of the lone researcher. Whatever the pros and cons of lone versus team research, the messy reality of the latter is certainly here to stay.

It may be that the loneliness of the sole researcher has simply been replaced by the difficulties of team work. For example, we have noticed how other senior colleagues share the tensions in hushed tones or in confidence – testament to the isolation of project managers, perhaps. As with so many aspects of the practicalities of doing research, such issues are seldom talked about up front and may be experienced as personal angers or failures by different members of the research team.

With the drive towards collaborative and interdisciplinary research, many of us find ourselves working in quite diverse teams. Here issues of status and power may be compounded by different disciplinary boundaries, paradigms and working practices. Research teams often operate with clearly demarcated roles and responsibilities, and there may be little attempt to develop a mutually sup-portive, egalitarian approach to the research process and its outputs. However, even when team members broadly share the same disciplinary perspectives and commitment to supportive team work, things do not always go smoothly. Through some occasional difficult experiences, we have become much more aware of the tensions inherent in any form of team working, no matter how supportive or egalitarian you might try to be.

During the past dozen years, we have 'managed' several different research teams, sometimes together, sometimes with others. While we still adhere to a supportive and egalitarian ethos, we have come to suspect that different team working approaches may simply mask rather than remove issues of hierarchy, status and power. Indeed, at times it has seemed that, no matter how hard you try, it is impossible to satisfy everyone's needs and sensitivities; it is a lucky team that finishes a project with all members happy to work together again!

We are not talking here about tensions relating to intellectual disagree-ments. Indeed, it is having just those sorts of discussions about substantive, theoretical or methodological issues that are the great bonuses of team work-ing. Our concerns relate more to the interpersonal relationship issues and sensitivities that we all bring to any group interaction. What are the things that make different team members feel cross (or worse) with each other – or hard done by? Ironically, such issues can be experienced as particularly difficult if you are trying to work on egalitarian lines, supporting less experienced researchers and sharing the intellectual life of the project. Despite your best intentions, the hierarchy can rise up and hit you in the face, with the result that sometimes you feel you cannot do right for doing wrong!

The positive aspects of team working are wonderful. The insights gained from working collaboratively on data are often greater than might have been achieved by an individual researcher. This often compensates for the fact that, as you become more established in academia, you are often more removed from the field. Discussing and analysing transcripts or field notes with the fieldworker can help to narrow that gap and bring a real sense of the 'field' back in again. Hopefully, for the fieldworker this leads to a less isolating experience. It also allows for both reflexivity and supervision to be built into the team effort, often resulting in higher-quality research.

However, team working is bound to be unequal, and qualitative research, in which not everyone is directly involved in fieldwork, raises particular issues. Although the benefits can be increased reflexivity and an opening up of the interpretive process in team meetings, this requires the sharing of fieldwork relationships and data. This may be experienced as intimidating by less experienced researchers, or by those working in a team context for the first time. How advice and suggestions are passed on and received may ruffle feathers all round.

Relatedly, different time commitments can lead to misunderstandings or feelings of being 'short changed' by a principal investigator's contribution. No matter how understanding and organized team members may be, it is almost inevitable that one or other member will at times have conflicting commitments that are inconvenient for the others, whether this be an overloaded grantholder who seems to be losing touch with the research or a contract researcher who needs to finish a PhD or start looking for another post, perhaps before the project grant finishes.

We have tried over the years to be as approachable and supportive as possible, believing ourselves to be sensitive to these and many other issues. At times, though, we have needed each other's support when we have either felt that we were not measuring up or that others were being unfairly critical of one of us. Very occasionally we have had to resort to sharing out the 'bad guy' jobs.

Although we feel that we are friendly and approachable, we have come to accept that others may find us intimidating – especially if they are new to research and worried about how we may judge their performance. Also, in some respects we may now take for granted our experience of working together over the years and have accommodated to each other's ways of working and idiosyncrasies. Kathryn is an inveterate and neurotic deadline meeter; Sarah often produces her best work right up to the line. Sarah has a streamlined approach to writing; Kathryn produces streams of consciousness! Nonetheless, we share a similar approach to the conduct, standards and outputs of qualitative research, about which we have never had a disagreement. Whilst we may regard this as a positive accommodation on our part, others may experience our 'united front' as intimidating, or fail to understand some of the implicit and taken-for-granted assumptions which we have developed over the years. More reflexivity required!

In our experience, personal and emotional issues are an inevitable part of team working and can seldom be put to one side. Good team working should be responsive to the needs of every member of the research team: it requires a sharing of information, an assumption of trust and a willingness to accommodate others' strengths and weaknesses. The challenge lies in balancing this kind of supportive and egalitarian ethos against the responsibilities of delivering high-quality research, within the time frame of a researcher's contract. Not to mention trying to retain mutual respect and good working relationships! Perhaps a clearer distinction is needed, from the outset, between those aspects of the research that are egalitarian (such as planning the study and working together on analysis) and those that are inevitably hierarchical (such as writing final reports, financial management, making decisions about the standard of outputs, whoever has written them). Denying the differing roles and responsibilities of team members is unwise and may only suppress open discussion of discontent, differences and ways forward.

Whilst concurring with Williams and colleagues that working with people from different disciplinary backgrounds can create particular challenges (and rewards), Cunningham-Burley and Backett-Milburn also show that individual personalities can have a major impact upon a team's dynamics. However, perhaps the most powerful feature of their vignette is the way in which they question the notion that team working can be – and should be – a truly collaborative endeavour. As they rightly point out, as much as we may like to wish/pretend that all members of a research team are equal, inevitably some members (such as project managers) are more equal than others. As they suggest, it is inevitable that different team members have different levels of power, status and responsibility, which can make it difficult – if not impossible – to foster truly equal partnerships.

As all the contributors to this section have demonstrated, working as part of a research team involves hard work. It requires us to be able to empathize with others, cater to their emotional and intellectual needs, respect their views and expertise, communicate our own needs and views clearly, and hone our listening skills. Whilst these qualities are not sufficient for successful team working, arguably they are essential qualities if we are going to work well together.

So you think it's all over . . . think again

Whilst gaining access to the field and fostering research collaborations throw up many challenges, these may sometimes pale into insignificance when we are faced with the task of disseminating our findings. In recent years, increasing emphasis has been placed upon dissemination practices. Many research sponsors/funders not only require our research to be 'policy relevant', they also expect wider public engagement with our research findings. Likewise, it is a certainty that our research participants gave up their time and invested their energy in our study in the hope that our findings will somehow improve the lot of human beings (the exception being those one or two extremely altruistic souls who are just keen to help us out). Consequently, research can no longer be confined to the ivory towers, for we are now seen to have a duty to engage with both non-academic and academic audiences. After all, our research cannot make a difference if nobody, except us, other members of our research team and those five people who attended our conference paper, knows about it.

So the data are gathered, analysed, written up, and maybe some have even been accepted for publication in an obscure academic journal. Now it is time to get the message into the public arena. There is one tried and trusted way of doing this – get the media interested. The down-side of this strategy is that it requires us to engage with journalists; a prospect that strikes fear in many academics' hearts. Journalists, as we all know, are the sultans of spin, the people who can twist our findings beyond all recognition. On the other hand, they are the people who can make our research count in a real way. When dealing with the media, we need to tread very carefully, as the three contributors to this section suggest. By sharing some of their successful and less successful experiences, these contributors provide some useful pointers for dealing with the media.

In the first vignette, Kay Tisdall shows how it is possible, with careful planning, to work with the media to ensure that our findings are disseminated in a sympathetic and (generally) accurate way. Focusing upon one study, which looked at violence amongst young girls, she describes how she and her co-researchers managed to control and, as a result, desensationalize media coverage of their research findings. Tisdall and her colleagues went to considerable efforts to ensure that the views of their young participants were reflected fairly in media accounts. However, in Tisdall's view, this did come at a cost. As she points out, so much adult intervention was required to protect the young people from potentially overzealous journalists, that it is possible that some of the girls may have lost their own voices in the process.

Participation or protection? Children, young people and dissemination

Kay Tisdall

Ensuring children's and young people's views are heard in all matters that affect them has become a mantra of children's policy. Childhood studies research emphasizes the need to recognize children as agents not objects, to represent children's voices, and to have children suitably involved in all stages of research. Most research funders now require that grant holders disseminate their findings widely, engaging the press, policy-makers and practitioners as well as academic audiences. But how do you involve children and young people sensitively in research dissemination, when the topic is almost invariably framed by stubbornly negative stereotypes and subject to media frenzies? My fellow researchers and I had to try to find answers to this question on a recent research project on girls and violent behaviour:[4]

We actually had been inspired to undertake A View from the Girls *because* of the media. In the late 1990s, there were sensational stories about the rising tide of female violence and the arrival of girl gangs in 'your very own local neighbourhood'. My colleagues and I were being telephoned as 'experts', to comment on these stories. But there was no systematic UK, let alone Scottish, evidence to which we could refer. We cited this in our application and, in due course, were fortunate enough to be granted funding.

The project prioritized the views of girls[5] in its methodology. Taking on board the arguments of childhood studies and children's rights, it argued that girls' views had to be heard in order to develop effective services, policy and practice. Anonymity in presenting the findings was promised to all participants, so that no names or specific locations would be mentioned in public materials. From the beginning, we knew that the media would be interested in the research – but then we were also interested in engaging with the media. Perhaps not as soon, however, as the media wanted to engage with us.

We received over 100 calls shortly after a four-line paragraph in the University of Glasgow's newsletter announced we had gained the funds for A View from the Girls. Obviously, there are some intrepid journalists who do read these university publications. Journalists wanted to run stories, following the usual stereotypes of girl gangs, young women on the rampage who were becoming more like boys. I have to deal with the press fairly regularly in my job at a national children's organization, where I am frequently required to put forward a view at short notice and comment on the on-going events of the day. But I feel quite different when I comment as an academic – you are being quoted as some kind of expert, which I presume should be based on some evidence. But the research team did not have any evidence because we had not yet done the research. That did not stop the press from wanting to report us: a headline, symbolic in its inaccuracy, read: 'Teen project looks at torture case' (*Greenock Telegraph*, 4 May 1998).

Once we did have evidence, we and our funder wanted to disseminate it. The project's dissemination plans included a high-profile national conference. And high-profile meant we wanted to encourage press coverage. So, we sought to plan our press strategy. It does not take a huge leap in logic to realize that the media are likely to have a different agenda to researchers. They are going to want something that is 'newsworthy' and thus grabs readers' attention. They are notorious for preferring quantitative over qualitative findings and are often accused of oversimplifying content and exaggerating the certainty and conclusiveness of research.

So, our press strategy was as follows. We organized an initial newspaper feature, so that our message would be out there first before any misinterpretation could take place. This was undertaken by a sympathetic journalist who was well briefed on our concerns about sensationalism. We wrote up a press release and sent it out. After hearing horror stories of journalists tracking down research participants and tricking them into thinking the research team had revealed their details (which the researchers had not), we contacted all our research participants' groups and let them know our dissemination plans. We particularly welcomed the opportunity to talk live on radio because it meant that our comments could not be edited substantially. And we sought to prepare for the inevitable question from the media: 'can we talk to children and young people?'

We had decided from the start that we would not ask actual research participants to present at the conference[6] but rather that we would invite a very similar group of girls to do so. This would protect the anonymity of our actual research participants. The girls presenting at the conference decided to work up a drama scene based on the themes we had found in the research. This drama scene depicted being harassed on a train in their local area by other girls. It went well. As so often happens, many conference attendees found the girls' presentation the most thought-provoking contribution of the whole day.

We were protective of the girls, spending time with them in advance of and on the day to try and highlight the potential disadvantages of speaking to the press – they might be misquoted or be depicted as 'violent girls' – so they could make an informed choice. We (the research team and the university press officer) spoke to the journalists before they met with the girls, and the press officer and a youth worker were with the girls when they were interviewed. The girls were told that they did not have to answer any question they did not want to. Overall, these girls reported feeling positive about their representation in subsequent newspaper articles. However, a few press items named individual girls and the particular neighbourhoods, and these girls were not pleased to have these represented as 'violent'.

Thus, I found myself caught in a particular irony: we as researchers may be critical of the 'hierarchy of consent', where we must go through several adult gatekeepers before the girls themselves can agree – or not – to participate; I promote children's and young people's participation in both individual and 'public' decision-making as part of my policy and academic work. But in this instance I was acting as a protective gatekeeper when it came to the media accessing girls who either participated in the research itself or in the conference.

In this case, the balance we struck was to facilitate the media's access to girls but not to those actually involved in the research. We sought to ensure that the girls presenting at the conference were informed, prepared and had adults to oversee the interactions between them and the media. Despite this, their media experience was not unproblematic, as detailed above. I still wonder whether there was more we could have done.

Overall, my media experiences were mixed. Positively, several journalists who attended the conference said that they had come with one story in mind and left with another – so we had hopes of some longer-term change in media representations of girls and violence (and, indeed, one reads far less of the standard headlines on this now). Negatively, I remain uneasy about how to involve children and young people positively in disseminating 'sensitive' research, and I feel (undue?) responsibility for how they are represented in the media. I may be angry if I am misquoted in the media but I feel a sense of responsibility if a child or young participant is.

I still refuse to believe that one cannot have media coverage that meets the journalists' requirements for newsworthiness and researchers' desire to have a fair reporting of their findings. After all, we did have some positive experiences and there was no problem in getting the media interested in such research. But changing a standard – and popularized – way of representing your research topic is hard and requires a media savvy that most research teams have had little chance to practise. Involving children and young people in research dissemination takes time and personal investment, and even then it can still raise ethical quandaries.

In contrast to Tisdall, who already had considerable media experience, Richard Mitchell relates what can only be described as a baptism of fire at the hands of the press. In his vignette, he describes an incident that happened early on in his research career when a local action group used the research he had been supervising to publicize their cause in a local newspaper.

A little local difficulty

Richard Mitchell

It was spring and I was in the second year of my PhD – a largely desk-based quantitative project, with occasional foray into the 'real world'. Spring also heralded the climax of a new undergraduate course in research methods designed and run by an enthusiastic and gifted young lecturer. Her social conscience and seemingly boundless energy had led to an arrangement whereby groups of second-year students were to design and carry out small research projects for local organizations and community groups. The idea was, as you can imagine, that the students would benefit from research experience founded on the skills they had been learning during the course. The various 'client groups' would benefit from the research results gained for free, but of a quality 'guaranteed' by supervision from departmental staff and PhD students. I was helping out with the course and a research assistant (let's call him Nick) and I were assigned to supervise a group of 15 or so students who had expressed interest in working on a quantitative project. Nick and I were very enthusiastic, perhaps because we shared the same dilemma in our research. Our skills lay in advanced, experimental, but ultimately desk-based, quantitative work and we yearned to do something which seemed more useful, hopefully with a health focus and well . . . preferably outdoors.

So, it was almost a dream come true when we were introduced to a community-based pressure group campaigning against a hazardous waste incinerator in their neighbourhood, a semi-rural area near Southampton. Let's call the group Worried About Pollution (WAP). WAP were specifically concerned about the potential effect of dioxins (allegedly) released into the air by the incineration process. This was an era when dioxins were rarely out of the news. Dioxins are small, highly stable particles rumoured to find their way into food chains and quietly build themselves into concentrations with the potential to do really nasty things to you. Those were the days when cows were still thought of as our friends and only politicians had heard of BSE; dioxins were environmental enemy number one. The possibility that high-temperature incineration could be a solution to hazardous waste management problems was being actively debated and vigorously contested by some. Sandals aside, WAP seemed to be a very motivated, intelligent and well-informed group. We were all quite excited.

It rapidly became clear, however, that WAP wanted us to provide evidence that the incinerator was causing health problems in their neighbourhood. They saw us as an opportunity to legitimate their concerns through the 'authority' which quantitative work is perceived (by some) to bring. Our first meeting set peals of alarm bells ringing for Nick and I. There was clearly a methodological mismatch between what we could manage to produce and the kind of questions WAP wanted answering. We knew we did not have the time, resources or inclination to pursue any kind of 'case and control' study looking for consequences of residential proximity to a point source of pollution. So, we explained quite firmly what kind of study might be possible and what kind of things it might reveal, stressing that we could not deliver a study which proposed or suggested any causal link between the incinerator and neighbourhood health. Surprisingly, WAP seemed happy enough with this.

I remember the project itself as fun and satisfying. There was the usual core group of students driving things along. Nick helped them build a profile of the neighbourhood from which we could derive an appropriate sampling strategy ('knock on as many doors as you can in two afternoons . . .') We helped the students design and produce their questionnaires using the software tools they'd been learning. The questions asked about perceptions of neighbourhood, individual and family health, as well as attitudes to the incinerator. When the fieldwork days came we were blessed with sunshine and no accidents or arrests. The highlight of the project for me was the cooperation of the incinerator company itself. After we had informed them of our research plans, they invited us all to look round the plant, see their 'information video' and interview staff and managers. We spent an afternoon there asking questions and nervously eyeing rusty drums marked 'POISON' or 'TOXIC'. I think we all wondered, even more than before, whether burning this stuff was really such a good idea. The company's public face was slick and squeaky clean. They were 'happy to co-operate', 'accepted the public's concern', but reminded us at every turn that there was 'no evidence' that their plant released dangerous levels of dioxins or that they caused health problems.

Data from the surveys were coded and analysed. Maps and graphs were drawn, cross-tabulations were produced, chi's were squared, the sample was (almost) representative and the results were clear. To be honest, I can't quite remember what the results actually *were*, but luckily this doesn't matter because the results themselves have no real part to play in this story. I do remember that a good proportion of people expressed concern about the incinerator and the health problems it might cause. They'd rather it was somewhere else – this seemed reasonable to us. The students wrote up the project, their energy flagging a little as we got closer to exam time and other coursework commitments loomed. There was a seminar at which all the student groups presented their results to the 'clients', and our students handed over a report to WAP after Nick and I had carefully vetted it for anything clearly libellous or too statistically awry. Summer arrived, the students left, a few weeks passed.

Even though I had seen the local newspaper's front page, I wasn't really expecting the phone call. The local newspaper was a free one and, whilst I don't want to cast aspersion on all free local papers, they are usually looking for a local story in neighbourhoods where newsworthy things occur rather less often than the newspaper is published. For this edition WAP and the local paper had gone to town with the study report. The headline was something along the lines of 'University study finds incinerator linked to community illness', and it was a *big* font. After reading their story I realized the headline might as well have been 'University proves incinerator kills families'. I also realized that the incinerator company was probably going to be a bit annoyed.

Their director spelled out the precise and considerable extent of their displeasure to me in the first few minutes of his phone call. I was alone in the postgraduate student office when the phone rang. The director did not lose his temper. He was quite calm. Calm in that 'first I'm going to toy with you, then I'm going to kill you' kind-of-way. Calm enough, in fact, not to mention that his company were going to sue the university, WAP and the newspaper until a good three or four minutes into the conversation. Actually, calling it a 'conversation' is a bit of an exaggeration. I sometimes got a chance to say something when he paused to breathe. I said things like 'I'm sorry', 'that was not what our study showed', and 'I understand how annoyed you must be'. Right from the start I could feel the threat of legal action heading my way. The fact that it took so long to materialize just made it all the more scary when he finally unveiled it. He was very sure of his ground and clearly used to defending his organization and its activities from far more solid challenges than this one (perhaps even those backed by real evidence). So, in retrospect I think my course of action was the right one; I apologized as profusely and as grovellingly as I could. Gradually the conversation crystallized around three key points. First, he was *really* annoyed. Second, I argued that we had been clear in our report that the study made no causal association between the incinerator and poor health in the community, that is, WAP and the paper had misinterpreted our findings by mistake or by design. Third, and this one seemed a long time coming, we were not really going to be sued.

In the pub afterwards (*very* shortly after opening time), with alcohol bringing some confidence back, I became convinced that since we had not agreed to the press release, and our report was clear in its findings, a successful suit against the university was unlikely. It also struck me that the director probably hadn't even seen our report in full. I wasn't so sure about the local paper's chances of defending its actions though, especially since it hadn't contacted us to confirm WAP's interpretation of the study findings. I wondered if my head of department and the vice-chancellor would agree with my legal instincts. I think Nick did phone WAP and some straight talking ensued, but they had achieved their aims. Their whole neighbourhood was, for a while at least, thinking more negatively about the incinerator and pondering what effect it might be having on their health. Probably no bad thing. WAP still exist today and continue their campaign against waste incineration. The incineration company has changed its name, but the incinerator remains there.

These events were certainly a lesson for me. We had covered dealing with the media in PhD research training, but not quite enough to deal with this! I know many academics who are deeply suspicious of the media and avoid contact with it at all costs. I suppose this story might provide them with greater resolve not to 'go public' with their work, but since then my colleagues and I have had research covered very effectively and carefully by the media. It can be a very effective means of disseminating findings. I also still work with community and pressure groups of one kind or another and have managed to avoid similar problems so far.

On reflection, I have three tips for dealing with the press. First, decide on the one or two crucial points that you want to get across and be prepared to make those points regardless of what you are actually asked (yes, the way politicians do it). It can be disheartening to reduce three years' work to one or two points, but if you don't do this the journalist probably will (and they'll probably choose the wrong ones). Journal articles and seminars are for intricate arguments. Newspapers, radio and television are for the 'big font' headlines. Second, consider it *your* job to make the story clear, not the press office's and not the journalists'. You need to be able to articulate what you did and why the world should take note of your findings, and I think practice is the best way to make sure you can do this. If you're going to be interviewed make a list of likely questions ('Why did you do this research? Did you expect to get that result? What do you want the government to do about it?' . . .) and practise giving concise answers, out loud. Third, make sure you write the best possible press release. Many papers will write their report based on that alone and won't bother to call you, so the press release is your main means of getting the message across. There are courses on this kind of thing. If your university or journal press office are going to write the press release, don't let them issue it until you are happy with it.

Finally, never, ever, do a press interview after going to the pub. I did this once and made a throwaway remark about Tony Blair's grasp of the north–south divide. It was reprinted in various newspapers the next day. Men wearing long coats and dark glasses have been following me ever since.

Mitchell's vignette clearly demonstrates that once our findings are in the public domain they can take on a life of their own. Whilst it can be difficult to predict exactly how our research may be used or abused by others, the very fact that other people can manipulate our findings should encourage us to adopt the kinds of proactive strategies that he and Tisdall recommend. We should also be mindful of our responsibilities to our research participants, and try to ensure that they are aware of our findings before they read about them in the press.

In the concluding vignette, Gillian Dunne describes her experiences of engaging with the media following her study of co-parenting in lesbian households. Like Tisdall and Mitchell, she argues that it is possible, even if we are hounded by the tabloids, to get a (fairly) accurate message out there. In particular, she notes the importance of being assertive when faced with journalists' more excessive demands. However, whilst most of her media encounters have been positive, she describes how it is possible for even an old media-hand to get caught out. The message Dunne sends out is that, even if we have years of experience of face-to-face combat with journalists, we should beware of being lulled into a false sense of security.

On not being on daytime telly or weathering a media storm

Gillian Dunne

There comes a point in the research process when you realize that something is missing. You have collected your interesting data, conducted your analysis, presented and published some scholarly papers, maybe even begun a book, but you still wonder what it was all about? Having immersed yourself in the lives of others, marvelled at the generosity of those who shared quite intimate aspects of their experience with you, you ask yourself, 'will my research really make a difference?'

Suddenly the telephone rings. It's a freelance journalist. He's read the Economic and Social Research Council press release on your findings, is fascinated and wants to know more. He is sympathetic, quite a radical and engages with what you say. You're excited – at last your stories will be heard out there, where it really matters. He rings you back to read through his article – it's great, on message. Later that evening, you get another call. This time it's a journalist from the *Sunday Express*. You had forgotten that your nice liberal freelance journalist sells his articles to the highest bidder. 'Can we just check through some details of this article', he says, 'and can you provide the names of some respondents so that we can interview them and perhaps take some photographs'. You say no to this second request, it's too sensitive an issue and you don't trust him. Eventually he gets to the main reason for his call. 'What about your personal circumstances, are you married, who are you living with?' You query the relevance of these questions, but fall back upon a status that will guarantee respectability. 'I am a widow with 11 step-children' you reply. Needless to say, your nickname at work immediately becomes 'Old Mother Hubbard!'

The next day you rush down to the newsagents to buy the paper. You assume that the absence of photographs and respondent interviews will relegate the story to the back pages. Shock, horror, you've made the front page. The banner headline reads 'LESBIANS MAKE BETTER PARENTS. FAMILY GROUPS ATTACK CAMBRIDGE STUDY'. Now you have learned that once it is out there, you have lost control of your message.

In many respects my research was rather conventional. Sure, it focused on lesbians, but it sought to investigate how women parenting with women resolved the contradiction between needing time to earn a living and time to care for their children. The study found that women parenting together solved this old conundrum by sharing the domestic, caring and paid work. I felt that the mainstream had something important to learn from these pioneering parents and that their parenting strategies were relevant to debates about the need to civilize the paid working week. However, in a bid to sell papers (despite a very thought-provoking and 'on-side' editorial) this message had been translated into a shock-horror headline that was guaranteed to inflame.

Following front-page coverage of my findings, my life changed dramatically. Over the next few weeks the phone never stopped. Fieldwork on my new project ground to a halt. I must have been contacted by every national paper, and some from abroad. Tabloid journalists hounded me day and night (being ex-directory posed no problem to this gaggle of sleuths). I was interviewed on the radio both here and abroad, and even visited by a German television crew.

While much of my engagement with the media proved very productive, I learned that the key to successful outcomes was an immense amount of selectivity. I found that before I could actually begin to discuss my findings, I had to engage in an uphill struggle to challenge the interviewer's frame of reference. Commonly, I experienced an intransigent naïvety in the media's homophobic approach to the topic. Ironically, this was often justified on the basis of 'of course I don't think this myself, but I don't want to alienate my audience' or 'we must give a balanced view'. Balance, in their minds, could only be achieved through the inclusion of some of the more extreme views of a 'moral majority' crusader. Thus, declining an invitation and not giving such views a platform was often the most productive outcome.

All this newly found media savvy did not, however, prevent me from making a monumental blunder. Just as things where calming down on the media front, I got a call from a researcher for a well-known daytime British television chat show – let's call it *RoyKing*. A whole programme, she told me, was going to be devoted to a discussion of my findings. The guests were all invited, and they needed me. What should I do? No one in their right mind would appear on this particular programme, but if I didn't, then what would happen to 'the guests' – didn't I have a duty to stand with them? I dithered. Finally, the director rang. He explained that he was a gay man himself. He said that this programme was going to be quite different – he had personally been involved in selecting guests. Several straight single mothers were going to speak about how they had joined forces with other mothers and how rewarding this had been. There would be a number of lesbian couples there to talk about their experience of shared parenting. This, he said, would be an important opportunity to challenge popular misconceptions. Thus said, I was persuaded.

A week later, a car arrived to take me to London. I was booked into a fine hotel, wined, dined and delivered to the film studio the next morning. Strangely, I was kept isolated from the rest of the guests. Conversations with the production team centred on my need to communicate in words of one syllable – my audience, I was told, should not be verbally challenged.

The time came, and I was led into the studio. I took my seat at the front and awaited the arrival of the great man himself – RoyKing. Lights, camera, action, applause, silence and then he spoke. 'Look, here, all of you. THIS IS THE WOMAN WHO TELLS US THAT LESBIANS ARE BETTER PARENTS, WHAT DO YOU THINK OF HER?' He pointed at me, and a collective hissing and booing filled the room – such was the intensity of the venom that, had there been rocks about, I would have been stoned immediately. My memory becomes blurred at this point. There were two lesbian couples – one woman valiantly tried to talk about their more creative parenting strategies – she was ridiculed. One parent in the other couple told the audience that she was 'really the man of the household and didn't like to get involved in "woman's work" '. The audience relaxed and felt more reassured. I remember too that an elderly gay man spoke out. He found the whole topic of gay parenting frightful, 'we shouldn't spread our perverted genes'. The audience cheered. I had been set up.

As my driver tried to console me on the way home, he felt moved to say that he thought there was a lot of sense in what I had said. He also told me that he had never seen anyone treated as badly by the *RoyKing* lynch mob – I obviously had touched a nerve. I am told that the director later resigned in disgust.

Once home I knew that I needed to do two things immediately. First, I had to inform as many people as possible that I had been set up, and had not willingly participated in such a programme. E-mail user groups and scholarly networks were a godsend. Second, as it wasn't a live programme, I had to prevent it being aired. This involved mobilizing any powerful bodies and people I had access to. This was a frantic time, during which I was put back together and re-energized by the kind words and support of the hundreds of academics and users who contacted me. The rest of the story is probably best left untold. Pressure was applied to the production team. To my knowledge the programme was never shown.

This all happened several years ago. That experience taught me to be much more careful in my engagement with the media, and media dissemination on my (later) research on gay fathers was generally positive, although there was one occasion when some of my research volunteers did experience a very aggressive radio interview. Again, the key to success was selectivity, and one of my greatest achievements was to be asked to co-direct a documentary about gay fathers. Interestingly, however, I have just heard that the media are after me again. I am able to screen the call. I am told that a production assistant from the daytime chat show *RoyKing* is keen to contact me. They would like to make a programme on gay parenting! I marvel at journalists' amnesia. They are told in no uncertain terms that I am off doing an exciting new project in South America.

Dealing with the media requires us to balance competing interests, namely our interest in getting our findings out there, the public's interest in receiving a clear and faithful account of the research, and the media's interest in gaining good copy. Tisdall's, Mitchell's and Dunne's vignettes demonstrate that this is not always an easy job. All three stress the importance of keeping control of our message and emphasize that, when it comes to engaging with the media, we should never let our guard down. Remember, as Mitchell points out, journalists are only in it for a good story and we do not necessarily want that story to be about us.

Working with others or working together

Taken together, the vignettes in this chapter forcefully illustrate that, despite the stereotype of the lone academic locked away in the library scribbling away furiously, social science research is rarely a solitary endeavour. From negotiating access to the field right through to publicizing our research findings, the impact and influence of other people is inevitable and unavoidable. Research in the social sciences necessarily involves a range of different actors whose competing interests frame and fashion the research process, for better or worse. Whilst it is not easy to satisfy all the competing interests and demands that we may face as researchers, it can be possible, but only if we keep an open mind. As researchers we need to be flexible, accommodating, and, above all else, prepared. And we also need to bear in mind that we cannot do this alone, for, after all, we are doing *social* science.

Notes

1   A Local Research Ethics Committee is a UK-based committee that is responsible for the ethical oversight of any research, in the local area, which involves patients or National Health Service staff or resources. In the UK, all research involving access to patients, patients' notes, or NHS staff requires ethical approval before it can commence.
2   There is smoking too, but not on the ward.
3   We are very grateful to the Wellcome Trust Biomedical Ethics programme for funding the project (No. 056009).
4   A View from the Girls: Exploring Violence and Violent Behaviour. Funded under the ESRC Violence Programme, Award Number L133251018. Others in the research team were: Michele Burman, Jane Brown and Susan Batchelor.
5   We were advised by girls in the pilot study to use 'girls' rather than 'young women'.
6   We did ensure that all girl participants were invited to the conference and received summaries of the research findings.

5
Control

Differences in status, power and control inhere in all kinds of social inter-actions, and research interactions are no different in this respect. Who controls the research agenda, and how control is negotiated, won, lost and regained may depend upon who has the greatest status and/or power, be this the researcher or our research participants. However, the authors of most research methods books assume that the balance of power rests with researchers – hence they emphasize the need for us to be sensitive to the potential influence we may exert over our research participants, particularly during recruitment or data collection (see, for example, Mason 1996; Silverman 1997). The vignettes in this chapter question this supposition by demonstrating that it is not always researchers who are in control (see also Lockyer, Platt and Tritter, Chapter 4, who highlight the control gatekeepers may exercise over our access to study participants), nor is it always necessary and desirable for us to be in control.

The contributors to the first section reflect upon instances when they felt they had lost control of their research by virtue of being deliberately or accidentally out-manoeuvred by their research participants. The vignettes in the second section, in contrast, describe occasions when researchers have deliberately tried to relocate the balance of power between themselves and their research participants by attempting to give the latter greater control over of the data collection process.

Who is really in control here?

With the exception of participatory research (see, for example, Whyte 1991), it is generally us who set the research agenda – we determine which types of data should be gathered, and how, when and where they are collected

(Mishler 1986; Mason 1996; Silverman 1997, Seale 1999). Or so it goes in theory. In practice, as the following vignettes reveal, things can be very different.

The section opens with vignettes by Marion McAllister and Elizabeth Ettorre respectively, in which they describe occasions when they felt they had been manipulated and/or out-manoeuvred by their research participants. In the first, McAllister reflects upon an incident which occurred during an interview study involving patients who were at increased risk of developing cancer and their 'at risk' relatives. McAllister was strongly reliant upon patients to approach and recruit family members to the study, a snowballing technique which was not without its problems. Recruiting relatives through patients meant that McAllister was not fully in control of the recruitment process, as the patients (rather than McAllister) had the final say over who they approached and how they explained the study to them. Indeed, after one particularly awkward interview, McAllister came away with a very strong suspicion that a patient had had her own agenda in mind when she recruited her son to the study, and that her agenda was very different to McAllister's own.

On being used by research participants

Marion McAllister

For my doctoral research I conducted a qualitative study of people's experiences of predictive genetic testing for hereditary colon cancer. I recruited clinical genetics patients who were at risk for a hereditary cancer syndrome, as well as some of their 'at risk' relatives who had not been to the genetic counselling clinic. Methodologically, in terms of dotting the ethical i's and crossing the ethical t's, I was well covered. I had medical research ethics committee approval for recruitment of 'active patients' through a hospital regional genetics service. I also had psychology research ethics committee approval to recruit their non-patient relatives, by family snowballing. Despite going through these committees, some ethically contentious events occurred during my research that neither the committee members nor I had anticipated.

Janice was recruited to my study through the hospital. She had a family history of cancer, and a mutation had been found in her family. Janice had had a predictive genetic test, which had revealed that she carried the mutation, and hence had a high risk of developing certain cancers in her lifetime. She appeared to be coping well with this. Janice told me that her brother had died from colon cancer in his 40s, twenty years prior to our interview. His wife, Catherine, and two young sons survived him. Both sons were at risk of developing the same cancer as their father, but, as Janice informed me, had not had genetic counselling. I asked Janice if her sister-in-law knew about the condition in the family, and the genetic test, and the fact that her sons were at risk. She replied that Catherine knew all about it. Janice also told me that her own youngest brother, Peter, who had also had colon cancer, had discussed his cancer and the genetic test with his two male nephews on more than one occasion.

Janice agreed to approach Catherine about participation in my study, so I left her a recruitment pack (information sheet, consent form, and prepaid envelope) to pass on. Some time later, I received consent from Catherine in the post. My interview with Catherine was relatively straightforward, and it was clear that Janice had indeed told her about the genetic test. In response to my questioning, Catherine also informed me that her sons knew about their risk, and about genetic testing. Afterwards, I asked Catherine if she would recruit her sons into my study, and she agreed. In due course, I received a consent form from Catherine's youngest son, John, who was in his late 20s, agreeing to take part. After obtaining consent from his GP, I arranged an interview.

When I arrived at John's home, I was greeted by a rather shy young man, who made little eye contact, and who seemed to be slightly agitated. We passed some pleasantries, and John seemed to relax just a little bit. He confirmed that he was keen to take part in my research, and he also agreed to be tape-recorded. My habit was to start my interviews with a very general question: 'Perhaps we could begin with you telling me the story, from your point of view, of what's happened in the family with regard to cancer, from when you first heard of anyone in the family being diagnosed with the disease . . .' In my experience, this is a good way to relax participants, and to get them to provide their own perspective on their family history and what it means. However, with John it quickly became clear that he wasn't ready to tell his story or to answer my questions, as he had too many questions of his own. He told me that he had read the information sheet for my study, which made reference to genetic testing for a hereditary cancer syndrome in his family. He also said that, prior to reading this, he had never heard of genetic testing, and had not known for sure that he was at risk of developing cancer. He knew that his father had died from cancer at a young age, and that other people in his family had also had cancer, but this had simply made him suspicious rather than certain about his own cancer risk. The information sheet had confirmed his worst fears. I was very shocked, because his mother had led me to believe that he knew about his risk status and the possibility of genetic testing.

When I realized the situation I was in, I lost all motivation to continue the interview. I felt that our 'contract' had collapsed and that I was there under false pretences. I told John that I felt uncomfortable because I had understood that he knew about the genetic test and his 'at risk' status. I was also concerned that John might want me to provide information about the condition in his family. However, he seemed keen to continue, and I felt I couldn't just leave him after dropping my bombshell. John did indeed have lots of questions, which, as a trained genetic counsellor, I could have answered. However, I was not there as

John's genetic counsellor – I was there as a researcher, and whatever ethical ground I had lost up until then, I didn't want to make things worse. I did tell John that the type of cancer his father had could be prevented, and that he could find out about that and genetic testing if he asked his GP for a referral to the regional genetics service.

After that (I think the word 'prevention' made all the difference), John settled down a bit. His manner remained very tentative, his speech was hesitant and his voice often trailed off before he finished his sentences. For this reason, I found the interview difficult, as it was sometimes hard to know what John was saying, or what he meant. One thing became very apparent in the interview – communication about his father's illness and death had been extremely problematic in his family. John told me that when he and his brother came home to spend Christmas with their mother, they never talked about his father's illness and death. However, his father's absence would hover like a cloud over the day, and at some point, year upon year, his mother would become tearful. I got the impression that John and his brother were never quite sure how to handle their mother's tears, and were paralysed by her grief, which perhaps meant that talking about their father's cancer became more and more difficult as years passed. John also talked about conversations he had had with his uncle, Peter, about the 'cancer in the family'. Although Janice had told me that Peter had made things clear to John about the implications of the family history and about genetic testing, from John's point of view, the conversations with Peter had not been so straightforward. John recalled a couple of 'casual' conversations, which had taken place during chance meetings with Peter in the pub, when the question of Peter's own diagnosis of cancer, and John's dad's diagnosis of cancer, had been raised by Peter. The impression I got was that John had been reluctant to hear what Peter had to say about the implications of the family history. John told me he had not wanted to 'go into all of that'. Perhaps Peter had found John hard to communicate with, in the same way that I had found it hard to know what he was saying sometimes as I interviewed him. In any event, John's and Janice's perceptions of the outcome of those conversations with Peter seemed not to be the same. The situation may have been compounded by 'Chinese whispers' in the family which led Janice (and perhaps Catherine?) to believe that John was up-to-date with regard to information about the family cancer syndrome and genetic testing.

At the end of the interview, I checked with John that it was OK to use the data for my research. He said 'yes'. I later checked with the regional genetics service whether he had been in touch with them, and to my relief, he had. I was also reassured by the genetic counsellor involved with his family that everything was under control. I did use the data from my interview with John in my analysis, and it ended up being very informative in relation to the impact of family communication difficulties on engagement with cancer risk in these families. Clearly, the communication difficulties between John and his mother about his father's illness and death had meant that John had *not* known with certainty about his risk, nor about the availability of genetic testing. Whether Catherine had meant to recruit me (perhaps opportunistically) to reveal this to John, rather than recruiting John to contribute to my research, I will never know. I did not find John easy to communicate with, and perhaps neither did his mother. Maybe they had had conversations at cross-purposes, and Catherine had *thought* she had made things clear to John. Or had Catherine seen me as an opportunity to put John in the picture, without her actually having to break the bad news to him herself, risking perhaps waking those demons that had haunted her family for so long? Whatever lay behind all of this, John obviously felt no ill-feelings towards Catherine for any part she had played – he said repeatedly in the interview 'She means well . . .' Perhaps he understood better than anyone what it might have cost her to bring the subject up with him.

As for John himself, what had his motives been? I felt he had wanted answers from me, which I hadn't really given him, but at least I had told him how to go about getting those answers. He clearly felt he couldn't ask his mother, and he hadn't wanted to 'go into all of that' with Peter either. In the end, I felt a little used by him (and his mother). Did I mind? At the time I did mind, because I worried that by raising this issue I had harmed John, and so I couldn't help feeling that somehow I had behaved unethically. But everything I had done, I had done in good faith, and two research ethics committees had approved my recruitment methods. In retrospect, I think it could be argued that John had gained something. He now receives the treatment he needs which can be effective in preventing colon cancer in men with a family history like his. So had anyone really been harmed if I had been used as an instrument of communication in a family for whom other strategies had failed? Arguably, Catherine, John and I had all gained something, even if the 'deal' had not been in line with my original agenda. So did it really matter that I wasn't in control?

Whilst McAllister was unsure whether she was deliberately manipulated by her research participant, Ettorre seems to be under no illusion. She describes an interview in which she felt out of control right from the start. Her research participant not only kept her waiting (an occupational hazard when interviewing busy people, such as doctors, in their workplace), but also proceeded to side-step the majority of her questions, preferring to set his own agenda instead.

Dealing with a difficult interview: professionalism and research ethics

Elizabeth Ettorre

In the autumn and winter of 1996, I visited a series of European countries in order to interview key experts working in the field of reproductive genetics. This research required much travelling and often I had only one week to interview experts (usually ten) in each country. While I had had quite a lot of experience conducting both structured and unstructured interviews over the years, I had never been in a position to interview well-known and, in some instances, famous individuals. (One of the key selection criteria for involvement in the study was that the expert as a respondent should be active and, indeed, visible in public debates in his/her particular country and thus have a public profile.)

My European research partners contacted expert respondents in their countries and asked them if they were willing to be interviewed by me. If they were interested and agreed, an interview time was arranged. I usually followed up my research partners' calls to the experts with a letter explaining how long the interview would take and what sorts of questions I wanted to ask. I would also confirm the date, time and place of the interview in this introductory letter. Given these experts' time constraints, I believed it was essential for me to alert my respondents beforehand about what would be required. I knew this was helpful in order to set the scene for the eventual interview. At the time, this seemed all pretty straightforward and I believed that I had a better chance of getting richer information if I let my respondents know what to expect than if I approached their interviews in a more *ad hoc* manner.

Looking back on this particular study, one interview inevitably comes to mind. It was probably the most difficult interview that I ever had to conduct. I'll never forget it. Whenever I think about it, I consider what I learned from the experience and refer to it as my 'bittersweet' interview.

It all began one weekday morning at 9.30, half an hour before I was due to interview one country's leading obstetrician (Dr O) in a large metropolitan hospital. I had another expert interview in the afternoon, so I had scheduled a taxi firm to shuttle me from place to place. As Dr O had not sent me directions of where to report to (which respondents usually did), I had added on extra time to enable me to find his office. My research partner had already informed me that the drive to the hospital from the hotel would be ten minutes and, sure enough, it was. However, when we arrived at the main entrance to the hospital, the taxi driver was unable to stop because there was a lot of congestion. Many people were being dropped off, presumably for appointments. The taxi driver took me to another entrance at the side of the hospital, which afterwards I realized was a service entrance. 'So much for hospital security', I thought.

Having made my way to the main entrance through a series of long corridors, I arrived at the information desk only to discover that it was not in use. In fact, it looked as if it hadn't been used in months, perhaps years. So, aware that the clock was ticking, I knew I had to fend for myself if I was to find Dr O by 10.00 am. It was already 9.45 am. I had 15 minutes. I began asking people dressed in what appeared to be hospital gear (scrubs, white coats) where I could find Dr O's room. Unfortunately, the first few did not speak English. Finally, one young male doctor did speak a little English. 'Dr O, yes, come this way', he said while directing me to the staircase. 'Go up to the next floor and you will find Dr O's office there'. When I arrived on the next floor, there was a queue of about 50 people who appeared to be waiting for appointments. There were no staff in sight. I waited for a few minutes. It was already 9.50 am. I was getting a little anxious because I always tried to arrive a little early to compose myself for the interviews. Finally, after a few minutes, a nurse came around the corner and I asked her where Dr O was. She said, 'Oh yes, Ettorre'. She directed me to a room the size of a large cupboard (which is really an exaggeration). The room was cluttered with books, papers and journals and also had a model of a women's uterus on a table, which was flanked by two chairs. I thought, 'Charming . . .' The nurse asked me to come in and said, 'Dr O is expecting you. Please sit here and wait for him. He is busy at the moment.' I was relieved to have finally found the right room and sat down to wait. It was 9.55 am. I waited and waited and waited, during which time I set up my tape recorder and arranged my papers. Finally, about 35 minutes later, Dr O arrived.

He offered no apologies for his tardiness. (He was 30 minutes late.) Saying how important his work was for his country, he quickly handed me one of his published articles on prenatal screening. I took the article and said, 'Thank you'. I was somewhat flabbergasted, but needed to get my bearings and ask for his permission to start taping before beginning the interview. However, I quickly realized it would be difficult for me to get a word in edgewise. He kept speaking about himself and his work. I kept nodding my head as I looked at the tape recorder. Finally, as he fiddled with the uterus model, he said, 'Oh start the tape, that is fine. I have no problem with it'. So I did and immediately said, 'Please, I want to tell you about the study' and went into my usual spiel. He interrupted me and said that my research partner had already told him about it. I thought, 'Good, he's been well prepped'. Then he said, 'But, what are you interested to know about me and my work?' I thought, 'Maybe I will still have a chance to ask my series of key questions'. The tape recorder was running and so I started working down my list of questions.

All went fine for the first few minutes until we came to the question about his views on prenatal screening. Somehow, with that question he took control of the interview. It was as if he wanted to impress me. After all, he was the expert, not me. But, unfortunately, he did the opposite. I was not impressed, but rather somewhat frustrated. Every time I wanted to speak he put up his finger as if to make me wait. After a few of these exchanges, I made the decision to let him go on and keep talking. I realized it was futile to interrupt him, for it was clear that he had his own agenda, so I relinquished control of the interview. But, as I began to listen carefully to what he was saying, I saw that what he was saying was a rich source of data – a minefield of information – and I was glad that I had kept the tape recorder running and let him take over.

His views on ethics were somewhat 'maverick' – you could say 'distorted'. For example, 'We make up our own ethics as we go along.' Most importantly, he held what could be regarded as ethically questionable views on how to negotiate amniocentesis[1] with 'his patients'. He stated his views clearly and concisely: 'If a patient does not agree to an abortion before we perform an amniocentesis, I won't carry out the procedure. We don't want any more disabled people in [his country].' Listening to him, I realized he was literally putting pressure on his patients into having selective abortions, whether or not they wanted them. I was somewhat startled. I had already read a substantial amount of literature about how this type of pressurizing, blackmailing even, was not only frowned upon, but also rejected by many practitioners in the field. Good clinicians, who see themselves as professionals, avoid this type of behaviour. The golden rule was the need for informed consent and to let pregnant women decide these things for themselves.

As my powerful respondent kept on speaking, I knew that while he had taken control of this interview, what was being chronicled on my tape recorder was an excellent example of those sorts of ideas perpetuated by experts who broke the rules and were, in fact, unethical or bad practitioners. He certainly broke rules in the interview situation as well as in his own medical practice.

In this sense, the interview taught me a valuable lesson: when people have disregard for rules, this disregard may come through in all sorts of ways and in all sorts of situations. While I may have found it difficult to proceed with this particular interview, I knew that it would inform my approach to other interviews in the study, as well as future studies. So rather than looking upon this interview as an example of 'interview interaction' failure, I saw it as a learning experience. Luckily, Dr O was the only 'bad practitioner' I interviewed in this study, although I was on high alert when another expert (a clinical geneticist in another country) tried to take over another interview. As it happened, he didn't succeed and my only explanation was that while he talked a lot, he still was interested in answering my questions.

While letting Dr O take control of the interview situation may have been a frustrating experience, it was also a humbling one. I was able to see that not all practitioners follow the correct professional procedures, although we tend to assume that they do, or at least give them the benefit of the doubt. This interview stays in my mind as an extraordinary example of a successful interview with a 'failed respondent'. My interviewee received 'low grades' in the field of professionalism and ethics, but I was the one who gained insights. He helped me to be aware of some of the ethical pitfalls that faced the experts I interviewed. They were not 'perfect', and having this 'bittersweet' interview experience just confirmed that awareness for me. Anyway, why should we expect experts to be perfect? They are only human too.

Whilst Ettorre clearly felt frustrated at being so comprehensively outmanoeuvred by the doctor she interviewed, she rightly acknowledges that the agenda he set himself (and her) was still pertinent to her research. Her experience thus suggests that, on occasions when we feel we are losing control, we should not despair, for allowing others to take control and dictate the agenda may produce some surprising, and indeed, useful, data (see Schwalbe and Wolkomir 2003). This is an issue to which we shall return in the second section of this chapter.

Ettorre and McAllister are not the only people who ended up in situations not entirely of their own making. In her vignette, Alice Lovell describes how she once found herself doing an interview with a woman who first bolted the doors of her house (with Lovell inside) and then proceeded to display increasingly erratic and threatening behaviour.

Tea and interviewing

Alice Lovell

One of the first interviews I carried out, nearly 25 years ago, was for a large research project which was designed to explore women's health and their personal relationships. It was a bright, sunny October morning when, with a spring in my step, I climbed the many flights of stone stairs up to the flat of my interviewee.

I rang the bell and Mrs S, a rather beady-eyed 52-year-old woman, peered at me suspiciously with the chain on the door. After a moment or two, she let me in and beckoned me to sit down while she closed the door behind me. She proceeded to slide massive bolts both at the top and bottom of the front door, put on the safety chain and turn the keys in the two locks. This multitude of locks and bolts chilled me and across my mind flashed the knowledge that nobody, but nobody, knew exactly where I was that morning. My colleagues and my family knew I had gone out interviewing, but only I had the address. This was in the 1970s, long before the days of the mobile phone.

I concentrated on the job in hand and banished these panicky thoughts, temporarily, from my mind. Mrs S asked whether I would like a cup of tea. During my training, I had been told that interviewees almost invariably offer refreshments and this is a useful icebreaker. It also offers the opportunity to get the tape recorder set up and to unpack the interview materials while the interviewee is pottering about with the kettle and tea things.

Mrs S was a twitchy participant, becoming highly animated to the point of belligerence. She smoked throughout the interview. Her answers were disconcerting and contradictory. When I asked about her family relationships, she told me she had a good relationship with her husband. She went on to say: 'I threw a cup of tea at him this morning because he wouldn't get up'. I became increasingly nervous when she admitted that 'yes', she did have a bit of a temper and had hit the man who came to demonstrate vacuum cleaners and had thrown a bucket of water over another man who annoyed her. She did not elaborate on what he had done to annoy her and would not be drawn.

Somehow I carried on with the interview, wanting my data, and because Mrs

S had clearly warmed to the occasion and was enjoying having a captive audience. She was not keen to answer my probing questions on my interview schedule, preferring to catalogue her complaints about her daughter and regale me with stories about her spirit guide, who appeared to her regularly.

However, the part of the interview that I found most chilling was in response to my questions about her friendships. Mrs S said that she kept herself to herself, but told me that she had at one time been friendly with one neighbour but that was all over now. Mrs S no longer trusted the woman and became suspicious of her to the point where she believed the neighbour wanted to harm her. She leaned towards me confidentially: 'She is trying to poison me by putting ground glass in my tea'.

At this point, I froze, put down my half-drunk cup of tea and, as she spoke, a cloud moved across the sun and the room suddenly became dark. Sitting there in the shadow, locked in with Mrs S, I felt as if I was in a horror film. I had quizzed Mrs S about her mental health, including asking whether she experienced feelings of unreality. I confess that she may have done but they were as nothing to the sense of unreality which engulfed me during that nightmare interview.

I still have the transcript, but it is an interview I shall never forget. After over 20 years, this interview has stayed fresh in my mind. Since then, I have added some hairy experiences to my research career. But none were quite as unnerving as what I mentally dubbed my 'ground glass' interviewee. I should like to say that from then on, I always left a note of the addresses where I was interviewing with family and colleagues, but . . . that would not be true. I did stop drinking the proffered cups of tea though.

Lovell's vignette raises pertinent issues about researcher safety, and, although it was not always a course of action she followed herself, her story does underline the importance of letting other people know our whereabouts when we are out in the field collecting data.

Whilst Liz Chapman does not have such an extreme story to tell, she also encountered a number of unpredictable (and seemingly uncontrollable) situations whilst undertaking home interviews for her study of people's experiences of living with HIV.

Drugs, drunks, dogs and dope, or taking the rough with the smooth

Liz Chapman

Between 1995 and 1998 I was engaged in PhD research which focused upon social support for people with HIV. This study entailed interviewing people living with HIV and their support partners (marital partners, parents, or friends). The research was specifically concerned with body image and how this might change once someone became HIV-positive and the effect that this might have on touch interactions between them and others. Consequently, the interviews included fairly intimate questions and the respondents sometimes became emotional.

Respondents frequently chose to be interviewed at home, where they presumably felt safer, being on 'home territory', so to speak. The homes I visited varied tremendously; sometimes they were bright and airy, on other occasions they were so dark (in one case the only light came from the luminous bubbling fish tank) that I had trouble writing my notes. Sometimes I arrived to discover a table covered with the paraphernalia of drug taking.

Many of the participants were HIV-positive because of their history of drug use, and many were still using. This meant I often entered households that were chaotic to say the least. Luckily, my previous 'buddying' experiences with an intravenous drug user had, to some extent, prepared me for this. But even so, I spent many fruitless hours travelling to respondents' homes only to find that they had forgotten our arrangement and had gone out.

The interview that I'm about to describe was pretty typical in that I turned up at the appointed hour only to find that the couple I was planning to interview had forgotten I was coming. Luckily they were in, but so was half the neighbourhood as well. On my way to their flat, ascending the dim, urine-smelling stairs, I could hear loud voices, a small child in what sounded like the throws of a vicious tantrum, and barking. Yes, they had a toddler *and* a dog! I must admit that I felt like turning around and going straight back home. My heart sank even further when I went into the main living room to find that there were at least three other people present, holding cans of beer (it was still before lunch time), who seemed very comfortably settled on the sofa. These 'spectators' were friends of the interviewees, two young men and a pregnant woman, and quite obviously, by the look of the overflowing ashtrays, they had already spent hours drinking beer and smoking. They didn't look as if they were going anywhere in a hurry.

After giving my spiel about who I was and why I was there, and 'surely you do remember we talked about this at the clinic last week' and so on, it all clicked into place and the interviewees said, 'oh yeah, sure, go on then, put your machine on . . .' I did suggest that they might prefer to do this in another room where it would be a bit quieter and more private, but they weren't having any of it. 'No here is fine', I was told. Although I would have been more comfortable doing the interview on a 'one-to-one' basis, I let myself be guided by the interviewees.

The first interview started terribly. The HIV-positive man answered just about every question in a glib fashion – if he could make a joke out of his responses (for the benefit of his drinking friends), all the better. For example, in answer to a question about his sexuality, he grinned and joked about how the size of his penis had not shrunk since he became HIV-positive, a comment that was met by gales of laughter from the assembled company.

Adding to my general unease and worry about the quality of the recording, both in terms of content and sound, the toddler (who was suffering with a cold) had several further tantrums and the dank-smelling dog growled and barked seemingly continuously (when he wasn't sitting on my tape recorder or pushing his wet, sticky nose into my bag). I struggled on valiantly. I knew that we were coming to the more difficult section of the interview, and that I needed to have my wits about me. But my brain was becoming increasingly addled by the dope that all the people in the room were smoking, bar the pregnant girlfriend, who was only drinking. Now we are not talking about a big, spacious, airy room here. We're talking about a small council flat with no open windows. Luckily, the passive dope smoking relaxed me a bit. I was able to see the funny side of all this, and rather than walking out and discarding the interview as a complete write-off, I stuck it out and chilled.

When we got to the really crucial questions, the man suddenly seemed to want to talk more seriously. He threw his friends out and started to concentrate on the interview. The questions that sobered him up related to his body image and how it had changed since he had become HIV-positive. Not specifically questions about size, shape or illness per se, but questions that made him think about whether anything fundamentally contaminating had occurred with the HIV infection. Given the amount he had drunk and smoked, he spoke very lucidly about his drug use and the contaminating effect that it (rather than the HIV virus) had had on his body image. Unexpectedly then, this interview ended up being very illuminating and produced some fascinating data that I am so glad I didn't miss.

So what can be learned from this story? When you are interviewing people who invite you into their homes, you have to be prepared to accept them and the way they live their lives. You have to sit tight, be flexible and open-minded. In other words, you have to be prepared to take the rough with the smooth.

As Chapman's story powerfully illustrates, letting our research participants dictate what is said and when it is said may still produce the kinds of data we both need and want. Thus she echoes Ettorre's message that when we find ourselves in situations where we seem to be losing control, we should not just give up and walk out.

Arguably, one of the reasons why Chapman did not feel entirely in control during her interviews was because these were undertaken in her participants' own homes. The implication of this is that Chapman was the guest in a setting where her study participants were the hosts; hence she had little say over what happened during the interviews and, indeed, if they happened at all. The idea that situational factors, such as the location of our research, can influence the amount of control we have over the data collection process is also vividly highlighted by Trudy Goodenough, who conducted focus groups with children in school settings. Goodenough recounts two incidents when she arrived at schools only to discover that all her meticulous forward planning had gone awry and that quick thinking and considerable improvisation were required to save the day.

Children's focus groups: location, location, location . . .

Trudy Goodenough

During the summer of 2001, I was involved in running focus groups with 8- to 10-year-old children. The purpose of these groups was to explore children's perceptions of health and illness and their experiences of involvement in research. In seeking the best location to run these groups, we considered several places, including community centres, our university centre meeting room, the children's own homes and schools. Finally we decided on schools because we wanted to give our research participants a sense of control – if we wanted to do anything, then we would need to ask the children or staff for information and/or permission. Using schools also meant that the children did not have to travel, nor did their parents/carers need to make extra arrange-ments for travel, childcare or to take time off work. Any compromises were to be made by us, not the participants, but we hoped that by detailed planning, in conjunction with school staff, any practical difficulties would be solved long before the focus group itself.

As with any research that depends on the goodwill and flexibility of others, it was important to meet key staff (usually the headteacher), and discuss what we planned to do in each school. This involved discussing what the children would be asked to do, and the type of space that we would require for the focus groups. We needed a space that would accommodate three researchers, up to eight children, video and audio recording equipment, as well as some room for the children to write or draw on worksheets, and eat a small snack.

I left each visit confident that the headteachers understood what we were attempting to do and that the physical spaces they had offered would match our requirements and would not be 'difficult' for the children to come to (for example we decided not to use the headteacher's office).

Reality!

Preparation is a wonderful thing, but even the best-laid plans need to be flexible. Prior to each focus group, we rang the school to make sure that they were expecting us, and that the relevant staff (class teacher, office staff and headteacher) knew which children were involved. We then gathered up armfuls of equipment: video camera, tripod, audio cassette, spare audio cassette, tapes, batteries, flat mike, three post boxes and cards (A4-sized), drinks, bis-cuits, crisps and fruit for each child (plus spares) worksheets, pens and pencils, and set out.

However whilst we may have been prepared, it became clear from day one of data collection that the schools were not always ready for us!

Perhaps the best example of this was when we discovered at the last moment that the room we had been allocated was still being used to dry 'play scenery', and thus was not available after all. The secretary took us on a tour of all other possible locations, including the staff room and an alcove connected to a busy corridor, before we chose the best option: a small resource room. Throughout this search, our focus group participants followed us around: not much chance to set up the equipment, and be ready and relaxed for the focus group!

The ability to think quickly and see potential in all spaces is a definite advantage in situations like this. Having a team of researchers working together is also a bonus, as the stress is shared. We resolved the physical space con-straints by leaving the post boxes[2] outside the room; wedging the video recorder and its operator high up amongst some shelves, putting the audio cassette and second researcher on the floor almost under the table . . . and the rest of us (one researcher and five children) sitting, under various resources, huddled around a small table with the rest of our equipment. After that there was little need to reduce power imbalances – the children could see that we were at the mercy of school arrangements as much as they were, and seeing us adults having to squeeze into difficult spaces may have helped them to feel we were all 'in this' together – and so we carried on. Plans to split the focus group into two were abandoned. Also the post boxes activity had to be held in the library/ cloakroom amongst pegs and lunchboxes. As the afternoon progressed, the room got hotter and hotter, and we all welcomed the refreshment break. Luckily, the children appeared to quite enjoy the challenges of camping out in such an odd place, despite the fact that some of the resources fell onto one of them (thankfully they were light!)

On another occasion, we arrived at a school and, although some people seemed to be expecting us, the headteacher had not remembered that it was 'today', nor which children were involved. We described (again) the sort of space we were hoping for, and listed the children we were expecting to come. We were initially offered the library, which was not a great location (and could be 'in use' while we were there). We were then offered a space on a mezzanine floor (next to the library) that was just the right size, had tables and sockets in all the right places, no direct sunlight and no low-level windows (so there was no danger that our focus group participants could be distracted by their friends in the play-ground). We agreed that this space was fine, and set ourselves up quickly. The children arrived and we got started. But as we began to record the group, we realized that the space was not as ideal as we had imagined; it was 'open' to all sorts of interruptions that we had not foreseen. These included: children run-ning a library club who wanted to come and see what we were doing; other children using the space as a short-cut between different parts of the school;

parents using the library space alongside for a book club who wondered 'when will you be finished?'; traffic noise from the local (usually quiet) road outside; and staff in the hall below dealing with children involved in lunchtime and play-ground incidents. We minimized the impact of these interruptions by diverting children away from the room, while two other children made a notice for us and put it on their classroom door to prevent 'short-cuts'. Other 'interrupters' were taken quietly out of the area by one of us, and given explanations about what we were doing and what we expected them to do. For the children this was to find somewhere else to be, and for the parents to come back in ten minutes when we would be finished, and could help *them* set up the library club if necessary. The children in the group were remarkably calm throughout all these inter-ruptions, and seemed able to concentrate on the task in hand. They seemed oblivious to the discussions below us, even when voices were raised in distress or anger. This was particularly impressive, as in addition to the 'physical inter-ruptions', we had discovered early on that the focus group clashed with a class treat (a fun afternoon and picnic). This added an emotional pressure – we needed to keep the focus group to time, so that the children did not miss out on the whole of their treat. Had we known that a class treat had been planned for that day we would have changed the date of the discussion group.

Whilst it is not always possible to predict how any physical space will alter a group's responses, in our experience, the negative effects of any location can be intensified or minimized by the reactions of, and interactions between, the children and researchers. It is up to researchers to be honest with the children, but at the same time to try to 'normalize' their experiences, so that they are comfortable in the focus group setting. We have found that events or situations that initially present as difficulties can result in benefits for the focus group. By providing a welcomed release of tension for all concerned, the logistical prob-lems we experienced served to reduce the unequal power relationship between us and the children. Perhaps the most important thing that we discovered was the importance of being (or appearing to be) relaxed, enjoying the challenges and being prepared for anything so that when plan A fails (as it frequently did), it is possible to quickly come up with plan B, C, D or even E. In other words, no matter how much preparation and organization is carried out, always expect the unexpected!

As Goodenough's vignette suggests, if our study participants have occasion to observe us during our more vulnerable moments this does not necessarily have to be a bad thing (see also Hallowell, Chapter 3). In her case, being seen by the pupils to be at the mercy of poor school organization may well have acted as a levelling device, one which, as she speculates, may have helped to put the school children at their ease in the focus groups (when these finally took place!) Sadly, Deborah Ritchie, Wendy Gnich and Odette Parry did not fare quite so well when they set up a focus group to look at young people's experiences of a smoking cessation intervention project. In their vignette, they describe the escalating chaos that ensued when their arrangements did not go to plan. They also highlight some of the pros and cons of using 'inducements' to encourage young people to take part in research.

We know what you did last summer!

Deborah Ritchie, Wendy Gnich and Odette Parry

Breathing Space was a smoking intervention project in a disadvantaged community of Edinburgh, which was evaluated using a quasi-experimental research design, and incorporated a qualitative element. Considerable effort had been expended in targeting young people and, therefore, we decided to carry out a series of focus groups to capture their experiences.

In one of these groups, we aimed to recruit young people aged 12 to 15 years who had participated in formal Breathing Space activities (including a smoking cessation 'poster competition' and 'designing a website' on smoking), as well as those who had had no formal involvement with these projects. Our intention was to recruit approximately eight young people to the group. However, because of our previous experience of recruiting respondents of all ages in this particular area, difficulties were anticipated. In an attempt to offset these problems, a number of measures were taken. These included involving community-based workers in recruitment (specifically individuals who had been involved in the running of projects associated with Breathing Space) and holding the focus group at a local and well-known venue. In addition, we attempted to 'woo' the young people with promises of £5 cinema vouchers.

The project workers wrote to Breathing Space participants, inviting them to attend a focus group discussion. The letter described the focus group as an opportunity for the young people to talk about what they had done during their summer holidays and encouraged them to invite a friend to the group. Much effort was put into the design of the flier that accompanied the letters and also the posters advertising the groups. In an effort to attract the young people's attention, the wording of a popular horror film 'We know what you did last summer' was used in the recruitment material. It also (for better or worse) served to deflect attention away from smoking, which was to be the focus of the group discussions.

In the event, the focus group was vastly oversubscribed. Whilst our anxiety levels were heightened initially because participants were slow, and in many cases late, arriving, eventually 40 young people turned up, eager to take part. It transpired that we had vastly underestimated the attractiveness of the free cinema tickets. Although we originally decided to provide each participant with two tickets, we had not intended to advise them of this. The local project workers, however, had assumed differently and the letter that they sent out promised two tickets rather than one. As a result, we had to turn people away and resorted to locking the doors of the venue in order to prevent the group becoming unmanageably large. Some of those who were excluded slumped on the doorstep crying and/or banged on the outside doors of the building, creating much mayhem. The noise they caused was exacerbated by the sound of bangers and fire crackers set off in the wake of bonfire night. While attempting to manage the group within the building, we had justifiable reason for concern about the safety of our (getaway) vehicle parked directly outside.

Participants were shown into a room and offered further inducements to remain – sweets, crisps and juice. At the outset, when the numbers were small, the majority sat quietly and politely refused anything to eat or drink. However, once the room neared full capacity, they all fell upon the provisions in a frenzied way and most of the consumables were demolished within seconds. As group facilitators, we could only stand by helpless and contemplate the daunting prospect of attempting to bring order to the escalating chaos.

Further difficulties occurred when we attempted to ascertain participant details such as: age, name, school and area of residence. It was suspected, and at times obvious, that participants were not answering truthfully, particularly when asked their age. The details they provided about themselves were continuously challenged by the other participants, and in this climate of escalating dissent, the group atmosphere deteriorated further. Although we did our utmost to exert control over the situation, it was clear that our authority was diminishing rapidly. We made a decision at this point to randomly allocate participants into two groups, which could be separated physically by at least one floor of the building.

So what went wrong? First, the group was much larger than anticipated, and still many young people had to be turned away. Some of those who were not selected became upset, and many were unruly and attempted to sabotage the groups. A group of girls who arrived late refused to participate when they witnessed the unruly behaviour of the boys. Keeping control of the group and maintaining a focus on the topic at hand proved extremely difficult. Participants were easily distracted. However, despite this, the strategy of alternately allowing them some slack and then regaining control of the groups yielded some fascinating data about smoking in the community. Participants were very candid about the Breathing Space projects and gave clear accounts of why they had or had not participated. These data were gleaned against a backdrop of shouting, joking, cursing and boisterous hilarity. On occasions, we resorted to switching off the tape recorder, threatening to leave the building and withhold the cinema tickets, in order to regain control. Of these threats, the latter was by far the most effective.

Second, because of the attractiveness of the free cinema tickets, information about the focus groups spread very quickly and widely among young people living in the community. As a result, some of those who arrived had neither participated in Breathing Space, nor accompanied a friend who had been involved. For these young people, the title of the flier, 'We know what you did last summer', was clearly misleading, and they wrongly assumed that they would be expected to talk generally about their summer holidays. This misunderstanding caused disruption, conflict and problems within both focus groups, mainly because these participants could not make a link between smoking and their vacation activities. Indeed, the extent of misunderstanding was such that some participants thought that we were actively promoting smoking, demanding to know, 'are you trying to get us to smoke?' and claiming 'that woman wants us to smoke'.

Third, because the groups were larger than anticipated, and because each participant expected to receive two tickets, there were not enough to go around. At first, we offered to take participants' details and post tickets to them; however, the majority had immediate plans for their tickets and those who were not fortunate enough to be selected (on a random basis) to receive a ticket on the night became extremely distressed. Because of this, we were forced to revise our plans and agreed to accompany those without tickets to the local cinema to purchase vouchers for them.

At this point, some of the young people demanded that we drive them to the cinema in our car (which was miraculously intact). Our refusal was met by a barrage of physical threats to our persons as well as the car. Moreover, the young people argued vehemently amongst themselves about who was most entitled to travel in the car with us. Upon arrival at the cinema, keeping order among this highly excited group, while staving off the disapproval of those queuing for tickets, was a stressful experience. The cinema employee who issued the vouchers demanded to know 'why are you doing this?' The question went unanswered as we looked forlornly at our entourage of 20 unruly young people and scrabbled for our personal credit cards to purchase a hundred pounds worth of vouchers.

We learnt several lessons from this episode. Our experience demonstrates the importance of having multiple facilitators, particularly for groups where order and control may be an issue. The laying down of ground rules, including, for example, the veto of mobile phones, is also advisable. In addition, clarifying the criteria for group inclusion with prospective participants is vital. Finally, if you do decide to use compensation for attendance, we recommend that this is not delayed or it may be viewed as a breach of trust. Although we found that the promise of free cinema tickets was undoubtedly useful for recruitment purposes, such inducements do raise ethical issues. It appeared that the desire to obtain tickets was greater than participants' interest and concerns about what they said, what was recorded and what the evaluation team intended to do with the data.

Ritchie and her colleagues are not the only people to have lost control whilst conducting focus groups: Jon Gabe has a similar tale to share from his study of violence in primary care settings. However, whilst in Ritchie, Gnich and Parry's case it appears that the sheer weight of numbers was to blame for the anarchic situation that emerged, for Gabe pre-existing tensions between individual group members may well have been responsible for the focus group 'discussion' degenerating into a series of personal recriminations.

Researching a sensitive topic in a heterogeneous focus group: the case of violence against members of a primary care team

Jon Gabe

Methods books on how to run focus groups advise that the more homogeneous the group is, the better its members will get on with each other and the higher the quality of input they will generate. This dictum seemed to be particularly important when studying a sensitive topic like the experience and management of violence against primary care staff by patients and the public – a topic that has the potential to generate strong feelings and opinions. With this in mind, my colleagues and I thought it would be desirable to set up groups who shared a similar occupation or profession and who were the same gender. However, we soon found that one's best-laid plans can come to nought when it comes to arranging focus groups with busy people who find it difficult to set aside an hour or two to discuss a topic which would have no immediate practical benefits, even if they were being offered a monetary reward for their services. We thus decided to compromise and run at least some groups comprising people from a range of occupations and different genders simply because it was expedient to do so. One such group was made up of all the members of a primary care team in a North London general practice – three general practitioners (two females, one male), one practice nurse (female), one practice manager (male), and two receptionists (both female). We expected that it might be difficult to get the receptionists in particular to participate because of their low status in the team hierarchy, but had not worked out any strategies in advance to deal with this possibility, preferring to run the group in the same way as all the others. The reality turned out to be rather different.

On the day of the focus group, my colleague and I arrived at the general practice, a converted house in a rather run-down area of North London, in good time to set up the microphones and arrange the seats before the planned start of 1:00 pm. We were ushered into an empty waiting room and began to think about how we could re-arrange things with the minimum of disruption, as we knew we would have to finish by 3:00 pm when the afternoon surgery was due to start. To our surprise, one side of the room had already been cleared and a table set with plates and cutlery. We had not been expecting a meal and started to feel increasingly favourably disposed to the practice for their apparent generosity. As the members of the team started to enter the room and introduce themselves there was a knock on the door. Outside was a pizza delivery woman with five large boxed pizzas, which were quickly taken in and opened. As we ate our food it soon became clear that this repast had not been put on for our benefit but for the GPs and their staff. We had unknowingly been eating pizza paid for by a representative of a pharmaceutical company who was also in the room. Aside from any moral scruples we might have felt, we soon realized that this meal was taking up valuable time that had been set aside for the focus group. As we were 'guests' of the practice, we had to wait (im)patiently as the prospective members of the focus group ate their pizza and discussed the latest medicine with the company representative.

Eventually the uneaten pizza was thrown away and the practice team sat down in a semi-circle facing my colleague and I. As there was no seating plan they could sit where they liked. They generally placed themselves next to a colleague with a similar occupational background. The receptionists sat in the centre of the semi-circle with the GPs, nurse and practice manager on either side of them.

Because of the lack of time, plans to use vignettes were put to one side and the focus group was run as a group interview. After everybody had filled in a short questionnaire about the level of violence in the practice and its management, we started to discuss what they defined violence to be and how it could be prevented. To our surprise the receptionists soon started talking, and indeed dominated the conversation in the early stages of the group. It became clear that they resented the way in which some of the GPs were not following the appointments procedure and were agreeing to have a consultation with a whole family in a ten-minute slot allocated for only one person. As a result other patients were delayed considerably and the receptionists had to face complaints, verbal abuse and even physical threats. The receptionists felt their attempts to follow practice policy were being undermined as patients bypassed them and took their whole family in to see the doctor.

As the focus group proceeded, the receptionists seemed to become more and more frustrated as the other members of the team appeared not to take seriously enough the levels of abuse they were facing on the reception desk. At one point one of the receptionists mentioned how she had been threatened with rape over the phone by a male patient. This drew an incredulous laugh from the male practice manager and an immediate response from the other receptionist, who turned on the practice manager and asked him 'Do you find that funny?' The practice manager immediately denied that he had found it amusing, but the receptionists did not seem completely satisfied with his answer.

The discussion subsequently moved on to the topic of preventive measures to minimize violence. While the receptionists and their colleagues all agreed that patients needed to be educated about practice policy as a way of reducing situations that provoked violence, the GPs and practice nurse also felt that staff needed to recognize that they too could be the cause of violence. This was like a 'red rag to a bull' for the receptionists, who replied bitterly that the doctors and the nurse clearly did not appreciate how much violence they were experiencing and that the 'patients are the source of the aggression . . . not us'. The nurse continued to express her view that staff should also be educated to understand the patient's point of view, supported by one of the doctors. At this point the two receptionists got up and walked out, ostensibly on the pretext of having to get ready for afternoon surgery, but clearly deeply frustrated at their colleagues' response. Feeling shocked and uncertain as to what to do, I decided as moderator to take my cue from the receptionists and call the focus group to a close.

As the above example illustrates, the mix of people from different backgrounds in a focus group does not necessarily mean that the less powerful will be silent or more reticent in speaking out. In groups where people know each other, and issues are being discussed about which opinions are strongly held, power differentials may be less important than the topic under discussion. The problem for the researcher in this situation is not how to coax the less powerful to speak but how to deal with the conflicts that may arise and the consequences for the participants, who have to continue to function as colleagues after the focus group ends. My belief was that the research had brought to the surface issues that urgently needed to be addressed by the group and had provided an opportunity to explore some possible solutions. Nonetheless, I was left with the uneasy feeling that while the focus group had generated some fascinating data, the experience for the participants had been unsettling and had raised more questions than answers. Responses to a short evaluation questionnaire, distributed after the focus group had ended, however, suggested that members of the practice had learned something from the discussion. And we heard subsequently that they had instituted a system for monitoring violence on their premises that had had some positive effect.

As all the vignettes is this section make clear, we are rarely in full control of our research, for the simple reason that we are so dependent on others to give us access or provide us with our data. No matter how hard we may try, it can be extremely difficult to second-guess their motivations for helping us, never mind anticipate (and accommodate) the conflicting demands they may have on their time. Perhaps the greatest lesson we can learn from these accounts is that in order to retain (at least) a sense of being in control of our research, our very best strategy may well be to be flexible, open-minded, prepared and, above all else, to always expect the unexpected.

Letting go

The contributors to the previous section unintentionally lost control of their research at various points and, in most cases, discovered unanticipated benefits as a consequence – such as getting good data. In this section, the authors describe their deliberate attempts to enhance the quality of their findings (and the ethical conduct of their research) and empower their research participants, by allowing them to exercise a fairly high degree of control over the data collection process.

One of the challenges all researchers face is how to ensure that our presence (as a researcher, with all that that entails) has minimal impact upon the types of data we hope to collect (Nash, Chapter 2; see also Finch 1984). As Virginia Morrow notes, this dilemma is particularly salient in research that involves young people, given that young people may be particularly anxious to please or impress (adult) researchers. Thus, in a recent project involving young people, Morrow tried to overcome the potentially biasing effect of her presence by employing a technique (photography) whereby she could be absent when some of the data were generated.

On not 'being there': creative methods in research with children and young people

Virginia Morrow

Social research with children and young people can be very exciting, but there are one or two things that researchers do need to think about. One concern, especially for researchers conducting research in schools, is that the children will try to please adult researchers by telling them what they think they want to hear rather than what they really think or feel. I have undertaken several pieces of research with children and young people, ranging in age from 8 to 16, and have often reflected on the way in which my very presence may influence the type of data produced. So when the opportunity arose for me to be absent during the data collection phases of one of my recent projects, I decided to give it a go.

The project: the 'official' story

In 1998–99 groups of 12- to 13-year-olds and 14- to 15-year-olds in two schools in a town in the southeast of England were asked to describe their neighbourhoods, as part of a wider qualitative research project investigating the relationship between health and social capital. The research used several different methods, including visual methods (map-drawing and photography), to explore children's views about places that they felt were important to them.

The previous paragraph is the sanitized version of the study design that appears in written accounts of the research, but what really happened, how did it work and what went through my mind when I was undertaking this project?

Working with children: reality

One of my main aims in the project was to elicit young people's perspectives on their local environments in a way that enabled them to choose and control what they wanted to depict. I knew from experience that drawing is less appropriate for older children; and that research needs to have an element of 'fun' in it to be appealing – so I didn't ask the older groups to complete a drawing task, but gave them cameras so they could photograph their localities. Ideally, I'd have given the whole sample cameras to use, but didn't have adequate funds, and this was a somewhat experimental technique, especially for the HEA, who were more concerned about where was 'my question about smoking'.

Thankfully, disposable cameras are cheap, so the project wouldn't have incurred a huge loss if they went missing (as some, of course, did). So armed with a bag full of cameras I went into school. I asked individuals and/or groups of Year 10 students to volunteer to take photographs of places that were important to them and then to describe why they had photographed the images. Some individual students took a camera and others shared a camera with one or two friends. The volunteers were asked to take about half a dozen photographs each for my research and I told them that they could use the rest of the film photographing whatever they wanted, and that they would be able to keep these extra snaps. I also asked them not to include people in the research photos, as I wouldn't be able to use them for ethical reasons.

After dishing out the cameras all I could do was sit back and hope that at least some would be returned. The cameras were returned sporadically, but I was visiting the schools regularly and this helped increase the number I received. The films were duly processed, and the packets of photos were given to the photographers unopened, so they could take out the 'non-research' shots. They sorted the photos, returned the research photos (about 100 in all) to me, and using self-adhesive notes, wrote captions on the back of each one describing what it was and why they had taken it.

Overall, working in groups and sharing cameras worked very well. There were, as might be expected, one or two problems – one girl complained that she kept forgetting her camera, and someone in another class grabbed it and took photos of the school roof and the ceiling. One boy was disappointed that some of his photos didn't come out (possibly the cardboard case covered the lens, he thought). In a couple of instances, young people mentioned things they had wished they had photographed but hadn't (for example, one girl, who had complained about a range of environmental factors affecting her neighbourhood and school, said 'I wish I'd taken a photo of the planes [that flew in low over the school], and the pylon in the school playing field'). Some of the children were very pleased with their photos, and although no one asked for copies of the research photos they all kept the negatives.

Adults' reactions

At the outset of the project I thought I might experience some scepticism from the staff with regard to my plan to use cameras. However, contrary to my expectations, the staff in both schools were tremendously supportive of the research and had no qualms about my handing out cameras to students. They could see the logic of trying to get children's perspectives on their environments through such a technique, and felt that while I might lose a few cameras, it would be interesting and worth a try. But it was in discussions over lunch in the local café with my colleagues and representatives of the local Health Promotion Agency and Health Action Zone team that speculations spun wildly out of control as to what would be photographed . . . Would they photograph something obscene? Would they photograph their bums? A great deal of banter and amusement was had over these speculations and, while I joined it, I gritted my teeth and thought to myself 'this tells us more about how adults view this particular age group than anything else'. However, this joking sowed the seeds of doubt in my mind, so when I took the cameras into my local photo-processing shop, I felt I had to mention to the staff that they were photos taken by 14- to 15-year-olds on their own, and would the shop kindly telephone me before telephoning the police if there was anything untoward on the films when they were printed? I felt embarrassed and silly doing this, and it proved to be quite unnecessary.

What are the pitfalls of using this method?

Despite the overall success of using this method of data collection it was not entirely problem free. One of the girls wrote a long description of her life outside school, and was eager to have a camera. She duly gave me her photographs, with written explanations of why she had taken them, but it was quite clear that she did not want to speak to me, and she said nothing in the group discussions. However, what she produced did cause me some concern. She described (in writing) how she wasn't happy with where she lived, and that, since she had moved about a year previously, 'I feel very upset because since we've been there, me and my mum have been having lots of angry rows'. She had photographed a number of cars, including her mum's car: 'I sit there if I'm upset'; and her nan's house, 'I chose this because I go there if I am upset. And I talk to her a lot.' In this case, because she did not appear to want to talk to me, I 'breached confidentiality' and mentioned my concern to her class tutor (who was familiar with her problems and was apparently providing support). But I was left with an awkward sense that the little mantra that researchers repeat about confidentiality when obtaining 'informed consent' with children and young people ('what you write/say/draw/photograph will be confidential to the researcher, but if you disclose something that worries me I have a responsibility to help, but I'll discuss it with you first') is quite inadequate in a case like this. Whilst this girl's anxieties and worries could just as easily have been elicited in a more conventional write and draw task, arguably allowing her to express herself using photography may have facilitated the expressions of these emotions.

However, with this one exception, the photographic exercise worked very well and everyone was pleased with the results – the photographers, school staff and myself. Indeed, since I have mastered the technological mysteries of the scanner, the photos have proved invaluable for dissemination purposes – livening up my PowerPoint presentations no end. Looking back, if I'd have known how well it was going to work I would have arranged to do an exhibition of the children's work, both the maps and the photos, and used this in my dissemination to the local authority.

Whilst removing ourselves from the field may be one way of empowering our participants, other strategies are also available to us. In their study of a particularly vulnerable group of research participants – homeless young lesbian and gay people – Shirley Prendergast and colleagues went to great lengths to enable their research participants to tell their stories in their own way. As Prendergast describes, this was achieved in part through the use of an innovative life-history interview method that was specifically designed for the project.

'Amongst the ranks of the vulnerable young': talking to young people about sensitive and painful experiences

Shirley Prendergast

That evocative phrase 'doing fieldwork' is a catch-all for what, for me, has been amongst the most complex, personally challenging and rewarding work I have ever undertaken. A very high degree of organizational foresight and conceptual and methodological preparedness must go hand in hand with a sympathetic imagining of the likely concerns, needs, feelings and responses of your respondents and an assessment (and possible re-alignment) of one's own presentation of self. All this is undertaken in an unfamiliar geography, at unusual times, whilst eating quantities of unsuitable food and in lodgings not of one's choosing!

Some dilemmas

Most qualitative research on social issues involves significant imbalances between researcher and researched. These may include their differential access to information and to the agendas underlying research, differential use of language and degrees of articulacy, unwritten assumptions about interpretation and translation, and lack of accountability and accessibility of completed research to respondents. Gill, David and I[3] came to our study of young homeless lesbian, gay and bi-sexual (LGB) people very aware of these issues. However, we also faced other equally challenging and complex issues in our fieldwork with this group.

First, we knew that our study would bring us face to face with extremely vulnerable young people who were negotiating difficult life events and daily hazards far beyond the experience of most researchers. Many had histories of abuse and abusive families and had experiences of being looked after in residential care from an early age. Many had experienced homophobic bullying and violence in and out of school, and some had run away or been thrown out of home because of their sexuality.

However, their difficulties were not at an end when they left their home town, since homelessness itself often brought on or triggered further serious physical, mental health and other problems. How were we to enable young people to talk about their lives without transgressing their privacy and personal boundaries? How best could we support them through any painful consequences which might arise from telling such stories to a stranger? Did we need support *ourselves* in undertaking such interviews?

Second, our theoretical approach to the issue of alternative sexualities was conceptually innovative. It challenged prevailing wisdom that these sexualities are *necessarily* dis-empowering and the prime causative agent of difficult life events. Put simply, while not ruling it out, we did not want to assume that being gay was always a disadvantage. What methods could we develop which were capable of exploring and recording both accounts of disadvantage and at the same time of encouraging reflections on individual agency and positive achievement, even for the most disadvantaged in our sample?

Third, we believed that any study we undertook should be capable of informing positive change. Bringing the experiences, wishes and needs of our sample to the attention of researchers and policy-makers was relatively simple and something which might help young people in similar circumstances in the future. But this did not seem enough. We were paid to collect accounts of ongoing painful and fractured lives, which respondents gave us for free with the promise of only distant benefit. Given the nature and scope of their difficulties, how best might we make participation in the research a positive and useful process, of more immediate value for participants themselves?

We resolved some of these issues by close cooperation with specialist agencies working with young homeless people. Using their premises, drawing upon their knowledge and skills, we (after a full police check) were able to meet our respondents in a familiar, comfortable but private setting. We spent whole days there, which enabled informal contact if anyone wished to talk after the interview, and there were friendly 'experts' on hand in following weeks. We offered hospitality with a shared supply of sandwiches, biscuits and hot/soft drinks, paid all travel expenses and made a small thank you offering of a Boots gift voucher.

Meeting the challenge: constructing a life-line

However, our most important innovation was the development of an adapted life-history approach to the interview which encouraged respondents to tell their story in their own way. Central to this was a visual 'life-line' to help young people reflect upon experiences as dynamic processes unfolding over time. In the best sociological tradition, this approach also resulted in other, unintended benefits. This is how it developed.

We loosely arranged our key interview questions into stage or age-related groups, for example, the primary school years, life at home as a child, the transition to secondary school, experiences as a teenager in and out of school, leaving home. Across these groupings ran common linking themes, for example: peer and parental expectations, fitting in, gender constraints, labelling of differ-ence, coping strategies and support. This structure had an immediate benefit in that it was logical and easy for us to remember whatever order it was done in.

We began each session by producing a large sheet of flip-chart paper and several coloured felt pens. Drawing a line right across the middle, we added a smiling baby on the left-hand side, made a mark in the middle and a smiling stick person on the right-hand side (our lack of artistic talent meant that most interviews began with respondents' barely repressed laughter). Noting that 'this was you as a baby, this is you at about the end of primary school, and this is you now' we invited our respondents to 'tell us about important moments and events in your life' beginning wherever they wished along the line.

Using different-coloured pens, we each added words, places, names and dates, funny or sometimes sad faces to the line. We made no prior assumptions about what was important or significant: narratives were respondent-led and we (carefully) followed. With both heads bent over the paper, constant eye contact was obviated and silent reflection was possible, crucial factors for people who are shy, or thinking about difficult things. Looking together, patterns might become visible, for example: 'There seems to be a big gap here between the ages of 11 and 16 . . .'; 'Yes, so much happened to me that year'; 'I had forgotten, s/he was a very important person'; 'It looks as though things are a bit better now.'

As our confidence grew we often managed to do our interview sitting on the floor around a coffee table. Although we always offered respondents a choice of male or female interviewers, we made another discovery – that when offered, some liked to talk with two of us instead of one. The friendly 'group' feeling seemed to allow them the space to gather their thoughts. Paradoxically, these sessions seemed to work well for people who wanted to take part in the study but who were very anxious and found it difficult to speak.

At the end of the session we turned the paper over. Continuing the life-line on the other side, we said, 'Now here is your life going on. Where do you want to be in five years, what are your hopes and dreams?' Our respondents almost always went on to project a time of greater agency and positive aims and achievements.

Reflections

This informal and holistic emphasis proved particularly valuable with young people who, we learned, had recounted the distressing and painful aspects of their lives many times over, to social workers, homeless agency workers and even the police, but who rarely talked to anybody about happier times, their achievements and hopes for the future.

Most crucially, learning about respondents in the context of their whole lives de-centred issues of sexuality. It would have been tempting to proceed as if their sexuality represented either a driving force in their life narrative or the cause of all their problems (sometimes it was and sometimes it wasn't). Instead, we provided respondents with the opportunity to talk about their sexuality within the context of their lives more generally: an opportunity readily taken up.

We cannot underestimate the significance of our more inclusive methodology for enabling the positive insights young people gave us as they told us their stories. As the interviews unfolded and respondents began to draw on a wider context and range of experience in the construction of their life-narratives, we believe that many were empowered as they began to reflect differently upon their lives. Overall we found the shared task of filling in and reflecting on these emerging stories to be a liberating, absorbing and inspiring way of working, for us and we believe for our respondents too. Moreover, the completed timelines remained as a vivid representation and visual *aide-memoire* of the interview that was invaluable in transcription and in so many other ways.

As Prendergast and colleagues found, allowing the research participants to set the interview agenda, with the minimum of prompting from the research team, produced some rich and diverse data and was perceived as an empowering experience by all. This vignette also demonstrates how important it is to 'break the ice' and make research participants feel safe and comfortable. Prendergast and her colleagues did this in various ways: hanging out with potential respondents beforehand, offering them tea and something to eat, avoiding eye contact or keeping quiet, offering them a choice of interviewer(s) and using amusing drawings. Some of these strategies were planned from the outset, whereas others emerged during the course of their study. Prendergast's experiences thus go to show that we cannot plan everything in advance; and, likewise, that in many cases it is little things that make all the difference to the success of our research.

Encouraging our research participants to take more control may have the effect of making research more reciprocal (Reissman 1987). However, on many occasions, the reciprocal nature of the research relationship is more apparent than real, for, after all, it is our research participants who give – they are the ones who account for their lives, express their emotions and share their stories. Researchers, on the other hand, take – we take away our participants' stories, experiences and views, and quite often we recast them to meet our own agenda (see Twigg, Chapter 2; see also Finch 1984). So how can we make our research have more than the appearance of reciprocity? This is a question that Tom Shakespeare explores in his contribution. Shakespeare describes how in the course of doing an interview with a disabled artist, he agreed to become the subject of this man's artwork. As Shakespeare concludes, by giving something of himself in return for the artist's participation in his research, he was able to 'balance' their relationship, making it more equal (see also Oakley 1981).

The art of representation

Tom Shakespeare

In 1994, I was one of a team who were commissioned to write a book about sexuality and disability.[4] We were three disabled people, with experience in campaigning and in counselling as well as in more conventional academic activity. We wanted to reveal experiences which had been largely invisible up to this time. The sparse literature on sex and disability was dominated by sexology and other medical discourses. Little if any of it was written by disabled people themselves. The disability movement, and academics working in disability studies, had been slow to act on the sexual rights of disabled people. The dominant materialist approach prioritized the public domain, not the private, and was suspicious of personal experience and life story narratives.

We set out to interview disabled people about their experiences of sex and love – what we called 'the good, the bad and the ugly'. The world of disability activism is comparatively small, and although we advertised widely for participants, most people we interviewed were known to us. Any research project involves questions of power and privacy, but these were increased by the sensitivity of the topic and the need to preserve anonymity around questions such as abuse or relationship experiences.

One man I interviewed was not bothered about anonymity. Eddie is a very direct, working-class man with spina bifida. He has a shaved head, an amputed leg, and an uncompromising commitment to disability direct action. He is also an artist. When I invited him to be interviewed, he readily agreed, but on one condition. He was prepared to answer my questions, but only if I was prepared to be painted during the interview.

I was delighted by the symbolism of this. It seemed to be a way of making the interview process more equal. He would be putting himself on the line by revealing his hopes and fears, and his rather chequered past. But I was also exposing myself, by allowing him to represent me in a portrait. As a person with restricted growth, I have not always been comfortable about seeing the way I look. Sometimes, I have found it hard to look in a mirror, or to see myself in visual representations.

Both Eddie and myself were putting trust in the other. He would faithfully represent me – not the superficial me, but the Tom whom he saw, and had got to know. I would do my best to record his thoughts and experiences in ways which were faithful to the Eddie I thought I knew, just as our book was an attempt to provide a balanced and respectful account of disabled sexuality in general.

It could be said that the best representation is a photograph, and the best narrative is a literal transcription. But I think sociology and art are about something rather different: both the researcher and the painter are telling stories, not showing things as they literally see them. A portrait by Pablo Picasso or Lucian Freud is revealing the subject as the artist sees them, filtering the objective image through a creative subjectivity. I want to do a sociology which tries to reach a deeper truth, a more literary or artistic representation, rather than bare facts or statistics. To do so makes the role of the author more important. But I think that the interviewer or writer in sociology always has power anyway. If we deny that power, then we kid ourselves, and our research participants.

We should be clear about the role we have, in selecting and filtering and interpreting information offered to us or gathered by us, and do our best to do justice to the people we work with. We should be humble about our responsibility, and ethical about our practice. For me, we need commitment to the individuals who agree to take part in our studies, not to the organizations that fund us or commission us. Emancipatory research in disability studies has stressed the controlling role of democratic organizations of disabled people: I think it is more relevant that we are faithful to the individuals whom we interview or observe.

When I went to visit friends, acquaintances or strangers, I was privileged to be allowed access to their most private thoughts and experiences. I interviewed people who did not share my sexuality, or my ethnicity, or my gender. I hope that most people experienced the process positively. Although there is often a suspicion of social research in political movements such as the disability movement, I think most people like to talk about themselves to a third party who will be non-judgemental, interested, and attentive. However, as interviews progressed, I would sometimes feel increasingly uncomfortable with the lack of balance in the situation. After an hour or two, I would have been told a lot of very private information, sometimes some shaming information, and certainly some information which perhaps few people in the world had heard before. So I tried deliberately to end the interviews by telling some of my story: naturally in the process of finishing the session, by chatting afterwards or, artificially, by saying that it was important to me that they had a chance to ask me questions too. If they had been open and frank with me, I wanted to even up our relationship by exposing myself also.

Eddie painting my picture was one of the times when the balance seemed most obvious. I think he was relaxed, concentrating on blending colours and planes to capture my unusual physicality, and answering questions almost as an afterthought. It made it slightly difficult to read my *aide-memoire*, and the tape of that interview has more pauses. After all, we were trying to do a number of different things at once: pose, question, paint and answer. We were both presenting our selves to the other. And, perhaps, this is what this form of social research is all about.

All the authors in this section suggest that by letting go – letting others dictate when, where, what and how data are collected – we can not only increase the degree of trust that exists between ourselves and our research participants, but also, as a consequence, we may collect better data. Whilst it may be difficult to let go, to give others more control or to give something of ourselves in return for their confidences, by doing so our research may have more than just an appearance of reciprocity. We may also feel better about ourselves and what we are doing in the process.

It ain't what you get; it's the way that you get it, and that's what gets results

Despite what many of the methods textbooks may say, research does not always run like clockwork. Even if we meticulously plan our research, we need to be inherently flexible when faced with the actualities of fieldwork (Mason 1996). Ultimately we can lose control of the situation at many different points during our research and in many different ways. We may be faced with uncooperative, unruly, rude or downright scary research participants (and/or gatekeepers); we may turn up at the appointed time to find they are not there or have invited their neighbours and friends in to watch; we may be asked embarrassing questions and our questions, in turn, may be ignored; we may be upset by the things we see or hear, or wonder whether we should break a confidence to protect someone else; we may be plied with alcohol or food we do not like and cannot eat, made to sit in sweltering or freezing temperatures, have to conduct interviews in a variety of unsuitable places and feel guilty for causing heartache and distress. All of these things may happen during the course of our research, and it can be extremely difficult to predict if and when they will occur. Indeed, as has been made evident many times throughout this and the last few chapters, research is hard work; work that can seem even harder if we lack the ability to empathize with others or adapt our research plans at a moment's notice.

Finally, as many of the contributors have indicated, the research relationships that produce the best results are those that involve the sharing of control, that is, they are based upon a degree of reciprocity between us and our research participants. Whilst absolute reciprocity in the research relationship may be a theoretical ideal, as these vignettes demonstrate, there is room for a degree of give and take. As researchers, we should not forget that all research involves implicit and explicit negotiation between ourselves and other people – gatekeepers, fellow team members, the media and, last but not least, our research participants themselves (see Gubrium and Holstein 2003). Ultimately, successful research, like tight-rope walking, is a balancing act – and whilst we may not break any limbs if we get it wrong, we could unintentionally harm our research participants or undermine the purpose of our research.

Notes

1 Amniocentesis is a medial procedure performed in the second or third trimester of pregnancy. Amniotic fluid is drawn from the amniotic sac around the foetus with a long needle through the pregnant woman's stomach. Because the fluid contains foetal cells, it is used to obtain genetic knowledge about the foetus. Amniocentesis can detect Down's syndrome, blood type, metabolic problems (such as Tay-Sachs disease) and neural problems. The results of this test are available within seven to ten days.

2 'One to one' confidential activity for children to evaluate topics raised in the focus group discussion.

3 The research was conducted by Gill Dunne, Department of Sociology, University of Plymouth; Shirley Prendergast, Department of Sociology, Anglia Polytechnic University, Cambridge; and David Telford, The Gender Institute, London School of Economics. We are grateful to the Economic and Social Research Council for funding this project entitled Making It Through: A Comparative Study of Transition for Young Lesbian and Gay People. Award number R/000/23/7995.

4 Shakespeare, T., Gillespie-Sells, K. and Davies D. (eds) (1996) The Sexual Politics of Disability: Untold Stories. London: Cassell.

6

Reflections on research: ethics in practice

So what will you, the reader, take away from this book? Some of the research stories you have read may have made you smile, even chuckle, brought a tear to your eye or made you yawn and skip the next few pages. Others may have made you sigh with relief: 'See it's not just me!' or filled you with trepidation about what might happen when you eventually get into the field 'Oh dear, that could so easily be me!' However, it's all very well reading about the scrapes other people get into and, undoubtedly, it is reassuring to know that you are not the only one out there who feels daunted, overwhelmed or exhilarated by what you are doing, or are about to do, but what does it all really mean?

Well, there is no easy answer to this question, but as we warned you earlier, this book is not just a collection of interesting, and sometimes amusing, anecdotes, it also contains a serious message. It is our contention that the stories in this book illustrate (implicitly if not explicitly) that research in the social sciences is first and foremost a moral activity. As the above chapters demonstrate, moral issues and ethical dilemmas can arise in multiple guises and at many points in the research process and, as such, they raise important questions about the need to maintain a distinction between research ethics on the one hand and research methods (research design, recruitment, data collection and analysis and so on) on the other. Well all that sounds a bit heavy so in these last few pages we will try to clarify our position. Hopefully, by the time you have read this chapter it will all become crystal clear and you will have come to think of ethics as fundamental to the conduct of research. If not, well at least you may have enjoyed some of the stories.

Research ethics: governance or bureaucracy?

Research ethics is now considered to be an essential aspect of research practice and a necessary part of research methods training. Current research governance arrangements in the UK[1] require that all research in the field of health care (both biomedical and social research) which involves 'National Health Service (NHS) resources' (a loosely defined concept which includes patients, staff, research conducted on NHS premises or that which involves recruiting participants using patient lists and so on) undergoes external ethical review by independent research ethics committees (local RECs or multi-centre RECs) (Department of Health 2001a, b).

Whilst there is no statutory requirement for non-health related social science research to undergo independent ethical review, an ever increasing number of universities and funders of social science research in the UK (for example, the Economic and Social Research Council (ESRC) and the Wellcome Trust) now require that the projects they accommodate/sponsor are subject to some form of ethical review. This has led to the development of in-house university research ethics committees (which in most cases are based on a quasi-medical model) who have the responsibility for ethical oversight of research with human subjects that is carried out within their institution. However, as Kent et al. (2002) have observed, in many instances social science research is not subject to institutional requirements concerning ethical review. In these cases, whilst the peer-review process, project advisory committees or research supervisors may provide a limited degree of ethical oversight, the ethical nature of research is primarily the responsibility of individual researchers – in essence, when it comes to ethics, a large proportion of social science research is self-regulated (Kent et al. 2002). Guidance in this respect is contained within ethical codes of practice issued by professional associations (such as the British Psychological Society, or the British Sociological Association) or research funders (such as the ESRC) who, in addition to emphasizing researchers' professional obligations, give advice about accessing participants and stress the necessity of gaining informed consent and maintaining participants' confidentiality.

On the positive side, independent ethical review not only functions to protect research participants' interests and well-being, but also potentially legitimates our research (Holm and Irving 2004). As such it may work in our favour by giving us the credibility necessary to facilitate our access to the field. Furthermore, as Holm and Irving (2004) note, the very process of undergoing ethical review – filling in those endless forms and meticulously detailing our methods – may increase the methodological rigour of our research. For if nothing else, it makes us stop and think about what we are going to do, why we want to do it and how we are going to go about doing it.

However, as more and more social scientists are beginning to observe, this preoccupation with research ethics or, more specifically, independent ethical review, may also have negative consequences for our work. The lengthy, and sometimes tortuous, process of obtaining ethical approval (see, for example, Silvester and Green 2003) has come to be seen by many of us as either a subtle form of research censorship (Kent *et al.* 2002; Lockyer, Chapter 4) or as a series of bureaucratic hoops that we, at times grudgingly, have to jump through before we are allowed to get on with what we want to do. Indeed, the growing insistence that all research on human subjects should undergo external independent review can be seen as changing the face of research ethics: it is fast becoming a bureaucratic exercise in form-filling. However, we believe that this bureaucratization of research ethics raises a far more serious problem. We suggest that as 'ethical approval' emerges as the supposed benchmark test for 'guaranteeing' that our research projects are ethical, research ethics is in danger of becoming removed from actual research practice. Research ethics is increasingly being seen as an 'add-on', a rubber-stamping exercise that we must undergo (with gritted teeth), rather than as an integral and ongoing aspect of our research. In this respect we would argue that bureaucratization is increasingly sequestering research ethics, and that the time has come to question this trend. But we are beginning to run away with ourselves here, so before we go any further perhaps we should back-pedal a bit and start at the beginning.

What is research ethics?

There are many good books out there that focus exclusively upon research ethics (for example, Homan 1991; Mauthner *et al.* 2002; Oliver 2003). Indeed, it has become such a 'sexy' topic that few research methods books fail to include a chapter on the ethics of research (such as Berg 1998; Bryman 2001). However, although the academic study of ethics has a long and illustrious history, interest in the ethics of research is a relatively recent phenomenon, emerging in the period immediately following the Second World War. The extent to which human beings were abused and exploited in 'quasi medical' experiments in the Nazi concentration camps, came to light during the Nuremberg trials. This led to the development of the *Nuremberg Code* in 1948 which provided the first set of ethical guidelines for research with human beings. This has been followed by the World Medical Association's *Declaration of Helsinki* (1964, latest revision 2000) and the Council of Europe's *Convention for the Protection of Human Rights and Dignity of the Human Being with Regard to the Application of Biology and Medicine* (1997), to name but a few. These guidelines promote the ethical treatment of research participants and the protection of individuals from exploitation and harm by advocating informed consent to research participation. This is evident in the following extracts from the Declaration of Helsinki:

10. The subjects must be volunteers and informed participants in the research project.

11. The right of research subjects to safeguard their integrity must always be respected. Every precaution should be taken to respect the privacy of the subject, the confidentiality of the patient's information and to minimize the impact of the study on the subject's physical and mental integrity and on the personality of the subject.

12. In any research on human beings, each potential subject must be adequately informed of the aims, methods, sources of funding, any possible conflicts of interest, institutional affiliations of the researcher, the anticipated benefits and potential risks of the study and the discomfort it may entail. The subject should be informed of the right to abstain from participation in the study or to withdraw consent to participate at any time without reprisal. After ensuring that the subject has understood the information, the physician should then obtain the subject's freely-given informed consent, preferably in writing. If the consent cannot be obtained in writing, the non-written consent must be formally documented and witnessed.

(World Medical Association 2000)

Whilst the requirements for undergoing independent ethical review may differ for biomedical and social research, in reality the guidelines for the ethical conduct of both types of research are very similar (Homan 1991). All ethical codes are concerned with a core set of issues, which include prohibitions against exploitation and exhortations to avoid harming research participants. They also emphasize the need to protect research participants' rights to freedom of choice and privacy. Thus, for example, the British Sociological Association's ethical guidelines (2002), like the Declaration of Helsinki, prioritize informed consent and confidentiality as follows:

16. As far as possible participation in sociological research should be based on the freely given informed consent of those studied. This implies a responsibility on the sociologist to explain in appropriate detail, and in terms meaningful to participants, what the research is about, who is undertaking and financing it, why it is being undertaken, and how it is to be disseminated and used.

17. Research participants should be made aware of their right to refuse participation whenever and for whatever reason they wish.

18. Research participants should understand how far they will be afforded anonymity and confidentiality and should be able to reject

the use of data-gathering devices such as tape recorders and video cameras. . . .

34. The anonymity and privacy of those who participate in the research process should be respected. Personal information concerning research participants should be kept confidential. In some cases it may be necessary to decide whether it is proper or appropriate even to record certain kinds of sensitive information.

(British Sociological Association 2002)

Arguably, then, research ethics in the twenty-first century is fast being reduced to the following prescriptions:

a) You should not subject research participants to any unnecessary (psychological, physical, economic, and so on) risks.
b) You should seek research participants' informed consent for participation.
c) You should maintain research participant's confidentiality.

Of course, we are aware that this list is a simplification of the myriad of ethical codes and guidelines that currently exist. However, in reality, when it comes to ethical review one could be forgiven for thinking that risk-benefit analysis, confidentiality and consent are the only things that matter to ethics committees or, indeed, to many of those academics who write about research ethics. Certainly, much attention has focused in recent years on the use of informed consent as an ethical guarantee (see Corrigan 2003). For example, many researchers have questioned whether it is possible, let alone ethical, to seek informed consent from people deemed to be legally 'incompetent', such as those with learning difficulties (Usher and Holmes 1997; Stalker 1998) and Alzheimer's disease (for example High 1992; Sachs 1998). Likewise, various researchers have reflected upon whether we can really assume that the informed consent given at a study's outset remains valid throughout the data collection process: study participants, for example, might simply forget what they have actually consented to (Munhall 1991; Lawton 2001); alternatively, (in-depth) qualitative research may go off in unanticipated directions, with the consequence that the study becomes something quite different to the one participants consented to take part in (Merrell and Williams 1994; Swain *et al.* 1998; James and Plazer 1999). The risks and benefits of taking part in research have been debated by social scientists especially in relation to their research with supposedly 'vulnerable' groups, such as patients with acute, chronic and/or incurable diseases. Whilst some have argued that it is unreasonable and unethical to bombard such patients with our research questions, particularly when they are feeling very unwell (de Raeve 1994;

Kritjanson, *et al.* 1994), others have questioned this seemingly paternalistic position by pointing to the benefits patients may gain from participating in research and from the knowledge that they are helping others (Raudonis 1992; Davies *et al.* 1998).

Arguably, the increasing preoccupation with risks, informed consent and confidentiality (demonstrated by both academics and research ethics committees) has the potential to lull us into a false sense of security when it comes to ethics, in so far as it suggests that these are the only things we need to really worry about if we want to ensure that our research is truly ethical. But, the reduction of research ethics to a few handy maxims, such as those outlined above, is only part of the problem. The assumption underlying the ethical codes and guidelines (and indeed, the very process of ethical review) is that the ethical issues that may arise during our research can be determined (and potentially managed) *a priori* (see Edwards and Mauthner 2002). However, in practice, this is rarely the case. Many of the situations we find ourselves in, or the ethical dilemmas we face, are difficult, if not impossible to predict at the outset, as many of the contributors to this book have demonstrated (for example, Thomas, Chapter 2; Williamson, Chapter 2; Potts, Chapter 3; and Platt, Chapter 4).

Thus, leaving aside, the question of whether it is possible to:

a) identify all of the potential harms which may result from our research in advance (see Twigg, Chapter 2 and Cox, Chapter 2), and consequently
b) gain truly informed consent from our participants (see O'Neil 2002; Silvester and Green 2003; Nash, Chapter 3) or
c) completely anonymize our research participants in our research reporting (Plummer 2001),

we do not believe that risk-benefit analysis, informed consent and confidentiality are the only issues we need to consider. Even if we could ensure that our participants really 'understand' our research aims/goals (Dawson 2003, and see McAllister, Chapter 5), we contend that there is more to making our research ethical than just getting someone to say 'yes'/sign on the dotted line or undertaking that we will never reveal our participants' identities.

Thus, we argue that whilst protecting our participants from harm/exploitation by gaining informed consent (and maintaining confidentiality), may be a necessary feature of ethical research, it is not sufficient for guaranteeing that our research is ethical. It is our contention that the ethical nature of our research is not just determined by ethical codes, ethics committees or, incidentally, our private intentions (for after all, we all *want* to do the right thing by our participants), but also by us behaving responsibly and with integrity no matter what is thrown at us during our research. But how do we ensure that this is the case? What counts as ethical conduct in the field?

The moralities of research: ending the sequestration of research ethics

> . . . moral conduct cannot be guaranteed by better designed contexts, nor by better formed motives of human action.
>
> (Bauman 1993: 10ff.)

In his book *Postmodern Ethics*, Bauman (1993) observes that one of the consequences of modernity is that morality is no longer seen as a 'natural trait' of human life, but as governed by 'man-made' universal ethical codes that are followed, or at least should be followed, by all 'rational' human beings. These ethical codes provide 'clear-cut' rules for our behaviour in a range of situations. As far as Bauman is concerned, this view of ethics is based upon the mistaken assumption that morality can be bracketed off from other aspects of human life (such as our emotions) and reduced to generalizable or universal rules of conduct. As he notes, conceiving of morality in this way '. . . substitutes the learnable knowledge of rules for the moral self constituted by responsibility' (1993: 11). In other words, morality is no longer seen as the province of the responsible self in its relations with others, but has become a matter of blindly following a set of arbitrary prescriptions, which predetermine what counts as moral behaviour. Bauman observes that, given the inherent unpredictability or ambiguity of human life, it is impossible to construct a set of ethical rules that could be used to enforce moral behaviour at all times and in all situations. He argues that we should see morality as a pervasive feature of all human activities and relationships, and suggests that we should adopt a position in which ethics is seen as a shifting and ever-changing phenomenon that is constantly subject to negotiation and renegotiation.

For Bauman, then, life is unpredictable and, as a consequence, morality is inherently ambiguous. Likewise, we would contend that social research, despite our rigorous planning, is similarly unpredictable. This being the case, we believe there can be no comprehensive set of ethical rules we can follow to ensure that our research is truly ethical (see also Homan 1991). Of course, we can *try* to predict the types of dilemmas that may arise during the course of our work and, yes, we can design our studies and procedures so as to minimize the likelihood of them occurring, but ultimately, we cannot always avoid them.

So if the ethical guidelines do not really work as well as we would like them to in practice, how should we conceive of ethics in social science research? As Plummer notes:

> We need stories and narratives of research ethics to help fashion our research lives, and to see the kind of broader principle . . . which they can

then draw upon . . . By and large, researchers do not follow binding universal rules; their ethics may draw from such rules but it surely applies them in situated contexts . . .

(2001: 229)

Plummer (2001), following Bauman (1993), argues that the ethical dilemmas we face during our research are situated dilemmas that require action and resolution not just theoretical debate. Thus, for Plummer, research ethics is not amenable to codification, it evolves and changes as our research evolves. Likewise, Birch *et al.* (2002) call for the contextualization of research ethics, for the grounding of ethics in real-life research practices. As far as these authors are concerned, what counts as an ethical dilemma or constitutes an ethical decision is not, and in many cases cannot be, determined *a priori*, but emerges in particular social contexts throughout the course of our research. But clearly, we can not just make up the rules as we go along, although it may feel like we do so on occasion. Like Plummer (2001) and Birch *et al.* (2002), we are of the opinion that the ethical choices we make as researchers are motivated by an underlying morality (for example, a desire to: respect and care for others; promote justice and equality; protect others' freedom and avoid harming others), which guides our behaviour, not just during the course of our research, but in all of our social interactions. Thus, we are not condoning a form of ethical relativism in which 'anything goes', for we do not believe that context alone determines the morality of our actions as researchers. However, whilst we do not see ethics as context-dependent, we believe that it is contextually sensitive, emerging from our interactions with others. Certainly, as the vignettes in this book have repeatedly shown us, when it comes to social science research, what counts as doing the right thing varies in any given situation – from project to project and person to person. As researchers (and human beings) we act as 'morally responsible selves' (Bauman 1993: 11) – we need to be flexible and reactive, but above all, accountable for our actions.

The research stories in this book have shown us that we, as individuals, are responsible for what happens during our research. Undertaking ethical research involves us making a range of decisions with regard to how we should behave towards others at all stages of the research process – before, during and after engagement in the field. These decisions are not just practical judgements, but moral decisions (which in many cases are driven by either our intuitions or emotions) about what we should do in a particular situation in order to achieve a balance between protecting our participants or ourselves and maintaining the integrity of our research.

Arguably, the most important message of this book is that our research is primarily dependent upon the relationships we have with others. It is the ways in which we relate to, or treat, others that make our research ethical.

Thus, in Chapter 2 we read about the important role played by emotions in our research, particularly how our own and others' emotional responses may be used to guide our behaviour when we are not quite sure of what is, indeed, the right thing to do. The vignettes in Chapter 3 focused on self-presentation and we learned that self-presentation not only influences the type of access we may achieve (and the types of data we subsequently gain), but also that being comfortable with who or what we are, or are perceived to be, is as important as making others comfortable with us. Chapter 4 stressed the importance of working with others to achieve our research goals, and emphasized the need for respect, empathy and flexibility in our interactions with those we encounter during the course of our research. Finally, the stories in Chapter 5 intimated that the balance of power which exists within the research situation is less clear-cut than we might expect. Whilst absolute reciprocity may be a theoretical goal, it is clear that we can not only give our participants greater control over the research process, but also that they, on occasion, may wrest control from us.

In essence, these research stories suggest that when it comes to carrying out our research, doing the right thing – the moral or ethical thing – is not always straightforward. Doing research can be likened to a fine balancing act. As researchers we need to balance our interests with those of our participants, funders/sponsors and, on occasion, those of the general public. We frequently need to strike a balance between giving our participants greater control (Morrow, Prendergast, Shakespeare, Robinson) and retaining some degree of control over our research (Ritchie et al., Ettorre, Dunne, Mitchell, Tisdall); between being who we are (Lippman, Hallowell, Bradby) and who we think our participants or collaborators imagine or want us to be (Eley, Barbour, McAllister, Horton, Kent); between being objective observer and subjective participant (Nash), expert and layperson (Potts), or friend and researcher (Exley, Robertson). We need to be flexible, accommodating and able to go with the flow, but at the same time not compromise our research (Goodenough, Richards, Tritter, Chapman, Gabe). We constantly need to balance our emotional responses with those of others, we need to empathize with our participants and co-workers, gatekeepers and other interested parties (Williams *et al.*, Cunningham-Burley and Backett-Milburn, Platt, Lockyer, Lobb); we need to emotionally engage but remain disengaged (Thomas, Williamson, Foster); appear uninvolved but be involved (Cox, Twigg); appear calm whilst raging or quivering with fear or excitement inside (Lovell, Grellier, Timmermans). In other words, as researchers we need to be all things, to all people, at all times *and* do this with integrity.

We finish by returning to our earlier question 'What is research ethics?' To repeat our prior observation, research ethics is not confined to ethical codes, the deliberations of ethics committees or to us having good intentions for that matter. Ethical research relies on all of these things and more. It is our belief that, in reality, there is no one thing that constitutes research ethics. To undertake ethical research we may need to: understand the ethical guidelines, gain approval from an ethics committee and have the best of intentions, but first and foremost, we have to be constantly aware of who we are, where we are and what we are doing.

To sum up, the vignettes in this book suggest that our reliance on ethical guidelines or ethical approval is not always enough to get us through the minefield of moral dilemmas that we may face when undertaking research. But whilst we endorse Corrigan and Williams-Jones' (2003: 2097) conclusion that we need to '. . . . promote [research] ethics as culture, not ethics as bureaucracy', we want to make it clear that we are not suggesting that we should ignore institutionalized ethical guidelines or refuse to seek ethical approval for our work, indeed, nothing could be further from the truth. However, we believe that the current arrangements for research governance and the increasing focus on a narrow range of ethical issues, such as consent and confidentiality, are in danger of marginalizing ethics. It is time to broaden our conception of research ethics, not reduce it to a handy checklist of procedures. We need to see ethics as an integral feature of all aspects of our research, from dreaming up a research question, designing the study, securing funding, negotiating access, recruiting participants, gathering and analysing data to reporting our findings. As the stories in this book have shown us, research, as a human activity, is a moral activity and all we are suggesting is that we treat it as such.

Postscript

Now whilst we have repeatedly said we do not think it is possible to produce a handy checklist of rules that can be used to guarantee that our research is ethical, the stories contained in this book do provide some handy tips which are worth considering:

- When it comes to gatekeepers, be prepared to argue your case, but be empathic and flexible. Do not forget that they may be aware of things that you are not.
- Be careful. Take steps to ensure your physical safety when you are out gathering data, for example, by telling people where you are going, what you are doing and when you plan to be back.
- Always have alternative plans up your sleeve in case things go wrong.
- Be kind to yourself. Do not try to do too much in one go – space out your interviews and/or take a break from fieldwork – you do not want to get burnt-out.

- Always treat people with respect – your sponsors/funders/gatekeepers/ research participants/co-workers/journalists. Listen to them.
- Be prepared to accept people's hospitality. Remember, when you go to other people's homes to gather data, you are their guest.
- Keep collaborators regularly informed, and make sure that the people who help you feel valued and appreciated.
- Be prepared to dress up or down as the occasion demands.
- Do not be afraid to seek advice, help or support at any stage during (and after) your research. Remember that it is good to talk.
- Be available and approachable so that fellow researchers/team members can come to you for advice and support.
- Tread carefully with the media/interest groups. Remember that their agenda may differ from yours.

And finally, ALWAYS EXPECT THE UNEXPECTED.

Note

1   For the purpose of this discussion we have concentrated upon the case of the UK, for an informative overview of the process of ethical review in the US, see Berg (1998). Readers should bear in mind that, whilst there are transnational guidelines (for example, the Declaration of Helsinki, or European Union directives) for the ethical conduct of biomedical research with human subjects, their implementation may differ across legal jurisdictions.

References

Bauman, Z. (1993) *Postmodern Ethics*. Oxford: Blackwell.

Berg, B.L. (1998) *Qualitative Research Methods for the Social Sciences*, 3rd edn. Boston: Allyn and Bacon.

Birch, M. and Miller, T. (2002) Encouraging participation: ethics and responsibilities, in M. Mauthner, M. Birch, J. Jessop and T. Miller (eds) *Ethics in Qualitative Research*. London: Sage.

Birch, M., Miller, T., Mauthner, M. and Jessop, J. (2002) Introduction, in M. Mauthner, M. Birch, J. Jessop and T. Miller (eds) *Ethics in Qualitative Research*. London: Sage.

British Sociological Association (2002) http://www.britsoc.co.uk/index.php?link_id= 14&area= item1

Bryman, A. (2001) *Social Research Methods*. Oxford: Oxford university Press.

Byrne-Armstrong, H., Higgs, J. and Horsfall, D. (2001) *Critical Moments in Qualitative Research*. Oxford: Butterworth-Heinemann.

Cannon, S. (1989) Social research in stressful settings: difficulties for the sociologist studying the treatment of breast cancer, *Sociology of Health and Illness*, 11(1): 62–77.

Coffey, A. (1999) *The Ethnographic Self. Fieldwork and the Representation of Identity*. London: Sage.

Corrigan, O. (2003) Empty ethics: the problem with informed consent, *Sociology of Health and Illness*, 25: 768–92.

Corrigan, O. and Williams-Jones, B. (2003) Consent is not enough – putting incompetent patients first in clinical trials, *The Lancet*, 361: 2096–7.

Council of Europe (1997) *Convention for the Protection of Human Rights and Dignity of the Human Being with Regard to the Application of Biology and Medicine*, http://conventions.coe.int/treaty/en/treaties/html/164.htm

Crossley, N. (1995) Body techniques, agency and intercorporeality: on Goffman's Relations in Public, *Sociology*, 29(1): 133–49.

Davies, E., Hall, S., Clarke, C., Bannon, M. and Hopkins, A. (1998) Do research interviews cause distress or interfere with management?, *Journal of the Royal College of Physicians of London*, 32: 406–11.

Dawson, A. (2003) Informed consent: should we really insist on it?, *New Review of Bioethics*, 1(1): 59–72.

De Raeve, L. (1994) Ethical issues in palliative care research, *Palliative Medicine*, 8: 298–305.

DeVault, M. (1999) *Liberating Method: Feminism and Social Research*. Philadelphia: Temple University Press.

Department of Health (2001a) *Research Governance Framework for Health and Social Care*, http://www.doh/gov.uk/research

Department of Health (2001b) *Governance Arrangements for Research Ethics Committees*, http://www.doh/gov.uk/research

Doucet, A. and Mauthner, N. (2002) Knowing responsibly: linking ethics, research practice and epistemology, in M. Mauthner, M. Birch, J. Jessop and T. Miller (eds) *Ethics in Qualitative Research*. London: Sage.

Dunscombe, J. and Jessop, J. (2002) 'Doing rapport' and the ethics of faking 'friendship', in M. Mauthner, M. Birch, J. Jessop and T. Miller (eds) *Ethics in Qualitative Research*. London: Sage.

Edwards, R. and Mauthner, M. (2002) Ethics and feminist research: theory and practice, in M. Mauthner, M. Birch, J. Jessop and T. Miller (eds) *Ethics in Qualitative Research*, London: Sage.

Finch, J. (1984) 'It's great to have someone to talk to': the ethics and politics of interviewing women, in C. Bell and H. Roberts (eds) *Social Researching: Policies, Problems and Practice*. London: Routledge and Keagan Paul.

Goffman, E. (1959) *The Presentation of Self in Everyday Life*. London: Penguin Books.

Gorer, G. (1965) *Death, Grief and Mourning*. New York: Routledge.

Gubrium, J.A. and Holstein, J.F. (eds) (2003) *Postmodern Interviewing*. Thousand Oaks: Sage.

Hammersley, M. and Atkinson, P. (1995) *Ethnography: Principles in Practice*. London: Routledge.

High, D. (1992) Research with Alzheimer's disease subjects – Informed consent and proxy decision making, *Journal of the American Geriatrics Society*, 40: 950–7.

Hochschild, A. (1983) *The Managed Heart: Commercialization of Human Feeling*. Berkeley: University of California Press.

Holm, S. and Irving, L. (2004) Research Ethics Committees in the social sciences, in K. Leonard (ed.) *Encyclopedia of Social Measurement*. San Diego, CA: Academic Press.

Homan, R. (1991) *The Ethics of Social Research*. London: Longman.

Hubbard, G., Backett-Milburn, K. and Kemmer, D. (2001) Working with emotion: issues for the researcher in fieldwork and teamwork, *International Journal of Social Research Methodology*, 4(2): 119–37.

Humphreys, L. (1970) *Tea Room Trade: Impersonal Sex in Public Places*. Chicago: Aldine.

James, T. and Plazer, H. (1999) Ethical considerations in qualitative research with vulnerable groups: exploring lesbians' and gay men's experiences of health care – a personal perspective, *Nursing Ethics*, 6: 71–81.

Johnson, B. and Clarke, J.M. (2003) Collecting sensitive data: the impact on researchers, *Qualitative Health Research*, 13(3): 421–34.

Kent, J., Williamson, E., Goodenough, T. and Ashcroft, R. (2002) Social science gets the ethics treatment: research governance and ethical review, *Sociological Research Online*, 7(4), http://www.socresonline.org.uk/7/4/williamson.html

Kleinman, S. and Copp, M. (1993) *Emotions and Fieldwork*. London: Sage.

Kritjanson, L., Hanson, E. and Belneaves, L. (1994) Research in palliative care: ethical issues, *Journal of Palliative Care*, 10: 10–15.

Lawton, J. (2001) Gaining and maintaining consent: ethical concerns raised in a study of dying patients, *Qualitative Health Research*, 11(5): 693–705.

Mason, J. (1996) *Qualitative Researching*. London: Sage.

Mauthner, M., Birch, M., Jessop, J. and Miller, T. (eds) (2002) *Ethics in Qualitative Research*. London: Sage.

Merrell, J. and Williams, A. (1994) Participant observation and informed consent: relationships and tactical decision-making in nursing research, *Nursing Ethics*, 1: 163–72.

Mishler, E.G. (1986) *Research Interviewing: Context and Narrative*. Cambridge, MA: Harvard University Press.

Munhall, P. (1991) Institutional review of qualitative research proposals: a task of no small consequence, in J. Morse (ed.) *Qualitative Nursing Research: A Contemporary Dialogue*. London: Sage.

Oakley, A. (1981) Interviewing women: a contradiction in terms, in H. Roberts (ed.) *Doing Feminist Research*. London: Routledge and Keagan Paul.

Oliver, P. (2003) *The Student's Guide to Research Ethics*. Maidenhead: Open University Press.

O'Neill, O. (2002) *Autonomy and Trust in Bioethics*. Cambridge: Cambridge University Press.

Plummer, K. (2001) *Documents of Life 2*. London: Sage.

Raudonis, B. (1992) Ethical considerations in qualitative research with hospice patients, *Qualitative Health Research*, 2: 238–49.

Reissman, C.K. (1987) When gender is not enough: women interviewing women, *Gender and Society*, 1: 172–207.

Sachs, G. (1998) Informed consent for research on human subjects with dementia, *Journal of the American Geriatrics Society*, 46: 8602–14.

Schwalbe, M.L. and Wolkomir, M. (2003) Interviewing men, in J.F. Holstein and J.A. Gubrium (eds) *Inside Interviewing*. Thousand Oaks: Sage.

Seale, C. (1999) *The Quality of Qualitative Research*. London: Sage.

Shakespeare, P., Atkinson, D. and French, S. (1997) *Reflecting on Research Practice: Issues in Health and Social Practice*. Buckingham: Open University Press.

Silverman, D. (ed.) (1997) *Qualitative Research. Theory, Method and Practice*. London: Sage.

Silvester, S. and Green, J. (2003) An excess of governance? Social research and Local Research Ethics Committees, *Medical Sociology News*, 29(3): 39–44.

Spradley, J.P. (1980) *Participant Observation*. London: Thomson Learning.

Stalker, K. (1998) Some ethical and methodological issues in research with people with learning difficulties, *Disability and Society*, 13: 5–19.

Swain, J., Heyman, B. and Gillman, M. (1998) Public research, private concerns: ethical issues in the use of open-ended interviews with people who have learning difficulties, *Disability and Society*, 13: 21–36.

Sword, W. (1999) Accounting for presence of self: reflections on doing qualitative research, *Qualitative Health Research*, 9(2): 270–8.

Usher, K. and Holmes, C. (1997) Ethical aspects of phenomenological research with mentally ill people, *Nursing Ethics*, 4: 49–56.

Whyte, W.F. (1991) *Participatory Action Research*. London: Sage.

World Medical Association (2000) *Declaration of Helsinki*, http://www.wma.net/e/policy/b3.htm

Young, E.H. and Lee, R.M. (1996) Fieldwork feelings as data: 'emotion work' and 'feeling rules' in first person accounts of sociological fieldwork, in V. James and J. Gabe (eds) *Health and the Sociology of Emotions*. Oxford: Blackwell.

RESEARCH METHODS IN HEALTH
INVESTIGATING HEALTH AND HEALTH SERVICES

Ann Bowling

Praise for the first edition of *Research Methods in Health*:

> . . . a brilliantly clear documentation of different philosophies, approaches and methods of research about health and services. Laid out in an accessible and manageable way, it covers an enormous amount of material without sacrificing thoroughness . . . I would recommend it to a broad readership.
>
> *MIDIRS Midwifery Digest*

> . . . This major research textbook is as good as an introduction to the field as you are likely to find.
>
> *The International Journal of Social Psychiatry*

> . . . an easy to read book with excellent background information on the theory and practice of research. A summary of main points, key terms and recommended reading follows each chapter and there is a useful glossary of terms at the end of the book for quick reference . . . I particularly liked the checklists when undertaking literature reviews and writing research proposals.
>
> *British Journal of Health Care Management*

This new edition of Ann Bowling's well-known and highly respected text has been thoroughly revised and updated to reflect key methodological developments in health research. It is a comprehensive, easy to read guide to the range of methods used to study and evaluate health and health services. It describes the concepts and methods used by the main disciplines involved in health research, including: demography, epidemiology, health economics, psychology and sociology.

The research methods described cover the assessment of health needs, morbidity and mortality trends and rates, costing health services, sampling for survey research, cross-sectional and longitudinal survey design, experimental methods and techniques of group assignment, questionnaire design, interviewing techniques, coding and analysis of quantitative data, methods and analysis of qualitative observational studies, and types of unstructured interviewing.

With new material on topics such as cluster randomization, utility analyses, patients' preferences, and perception of risk, the text is aimed at students and researchers of health and health services. It has also been designed for health professionals and policy makers who have responsibility for applying research findings in practice, and who need to know how to judge the value of that research.

Contents

512pp   0 335 20643 3 (Paperback)   0 335 20644 1 (Hardback)

QUALITATIVE RESEARCH IN PRACTICE
STORIES FROM THE FIELD

Yvonne Darlington and Dorothy Scott

Qualitative Research in Practice is a book we have all been waiting for. The authors have shared with us their stories about the qualitative research process while linking their experiences to theory and practice in human services. The difficulties, successes and new pathways created by their research findings shed new light on the complex journey qualitative researchers embark on with every new research project.

Professor Gay Edgecombe, Director of International Studies for
Nursing and Public Health, RMIT University, Australia

I would recommend this book to my students at undergraduate and postgraduate levels. I believe that after reading this book, students will no longer be frightened by qualitative research and will have an interest and enthusiasm in trying it out.

Professor Joyce L.C. Ma, Department of Social Work,
The Chinese University of Hong Kong

Qualitative Research in Practice bridges the gap between theory and practice in research, and between the academic and practice contexts in the human services. The focus is on 'doing' research and 'being' a researcher, rather than on 'how to do' research.

The authors provide an introduction to qualitative research through actual research projects that illustrate key stages in the research process. They draw on experiences of research undertaken in a variety of human service areas by researchers in Australia, the UK, New Zealand and Hong Kong. These 'stories from the field' are framed by broader discussions by the authors of the research process.

The researchers' stories reveal the human face of research undertaken in often difficult contexts: with homeless people, with disabled people, in nursing homes, with victims of domestic violence, and with adopted children. We see how these researchers have dealt with the many obstacles they faced in their research projects, and how they developed innovative solutions.

Qualitative Research in Practice is a collection of 'practice wisdom' that makes an ideal companion to conventional research methods texts for students and practitioners doing research in social work, welfare, community health, counselling and related fields.

Contents

224pp   0 335 21147 X (Paperback)

EVIDENCE-BASED RESEARCH
DILEMMAS AND DEBATES IN HEALTH CARE

Brian Brown, Paul Crawford and Carolyn Hicks

- Why is the philosophy of science important for health care research?
- What impact do world-views and paradigms have on the research process and the knowledge it generates?
- Why do some kinds of concepts get replaced by others?

This book covers the major perspectives in the philosophy of science and critically discusses their relevance to health care research, using examples of paradigms, concepts, theories and research findings in the health sciences. It makes sense of the bewildering variety of assumptions, world-views and epistemological implications of the different research methods. It enables the reader to become an informed consumer of scholarship on health care issues.

The authors describe how health care research has been influenced by positivistic and interpretative approaches, and how it has recently been challenged by postmodernist philosophies. All of these approaches have research methods aligned with them which have taken their place in the panoply of tools at the disposal of the health scientist.

Written in a clear and accessible style, *Evidence-Based Research* demonstrates how the different philosophical bases to research impact in real-life health care work and research. It is key reading for the growing number of people involved in health care research in universities and health settings, and is particularly suitable for advanced undergraduate and masters students researching in the health care sciences.

Contents

Introduction: theories of science and theories of society – Epistemology I: positivism – 'they don't build epistemologies like that any more' – Concepts and theories I: what is a concept in the health sciences? – Concepts and theories II: operationalism and its legacy – The philosophy of experimentation – Experiments in medicine and the health sciences – Epistemology II: interpretation and hermeneutics – Philosophies of description – The post-modernist challenge – Philosophy and research design in practice – References – Index.

312pp   0 335 21164 X (Paperback)   0 335 21165 8 (Hardback)

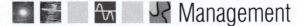